The Imperative Quest
To Freedom

Michele Doucette, M. Ed.

The Imperative Quest To Freedom

ISBN 978-1-935786-60-3

Printed in the United States of America by

St. Clair Publications

PO Box 726

McMinnville, TN   37111-0726

stclairpublications.com

Table of Contents

As Osho has stated ...... *The real mystic is so utterly absorbed by the present that he has no time, no energy, for the past and the future; they don't live for any ideal, and they don't live against any ideal. The sheer purity of this moment: they live it, they enjoy it, they sing it, they dance it. And when the next moment comes, they live the next moment with the same joy, with the same cheerfulness.*

Prologue

A lofty and often overused term, freedom is one that we believe adheres to us; a form of divine right, if you will.

I am a believer in the freedom that allows me to make my own choices, and live my own life, as long as I *do not infringe upon the rights of others*, through such means as violence, slavery, persecution, subordination, dominance, power and control.

Unfortunately, society, by its very nature, always seeks to conform the individual, to control the individual, to think for the individual, meaning that society, as both a created and collective body, also infringes upon the inherent rights of all.

In short, you can either accept the choices (decisions) that are being made for you or you can you emerge with bravery, with tenacity, with determination, to make your own choices (decisions), thereby taking full ownership and responsibility for the choices (decisions) that are made.

A Very Special Dedication

James Clark Robbins, known to me as cousin Clark, was supportive of every project that I undertook, be it genealogy or otherwise.

When I would talk to him about my difficult teaching assignment, working with Pervasive Needs students, he would sit me down and say ...... *Michèle, you are strong. If you can survive these challenging students, and these difficult situations, you can survive anything.*

Transitioning to the spiritual realm in the early hours of Monday, September 21, 2015, Clark would have celebrated his 73rd birthday on Saturday, September 26, 2015. Instead, this was the day that was chosen as his memorial service; an apt day to celebrate his life.

Despite my having retired, the end of June 2016, after 31 years as a Special Education Teacher, I still miss his staunch, unfailing and unwavering support.

Dedicated to him, this book speaks to his enthusiasm and zest for life.

Câlins et Bisous .... ♥

Further Acknowledgments

Into The Sunset is the artwork featured on the cover of this book. John Robichaud (www.JohnRobichaud.com) is the gifted artist. I would also encourage you to check out his remarkable page on Facebook. [1]

To share John's words ......

I am drawn to the power of the Inukshuk. Traditionally, the Inuit people created these stone likenesses of the human form to mark their passing presence in a place (symbolizing we were here) or to act as a guide post or marker for a traveler (with a message to indicate you have not lost your way). Both would have been welcome and comforting messages in the harsh and largely empty high northern landscape. So simply constructed, yet so effective; each executed with a touch of artistic flare belonging to its creator.

---

[1] https://www.facebook.com/John-Robichaud-photographer-artist-filmmaker-343159522401877/

This example is neither in the high north nor is it likely that it was built by an Inuit person, but, still, the power of the structure and its human form resonates.

Thank you to whoever built this Inukshuk on the dykelands surrounding Wolfville, Nova Scotia. It made for a perfect opportunity to capture the setting sun over the Bay of Fundy as it lit the heart of this stationary traveler.

I can imagine a very similar scene being repeated across the arctic, countless times over millennia; the low northern sun illuminating and warming these lone figures as they perform their solitary duty.

I see this as a most fitting tribute to all who are beckoned, who are summoned, who are commanded, by the imperative quest to freedom. As you can see, you have not lost your way, for you, too, are here.

May this particular Inukshuk serve you, the reader, well.

The Quest for Freedom

As long as you allow yourself to exist as a mindless drone of the collective, you are suppressing your ability to think freely, you are suppressing your ability to think consciously, you are suppressing your ability to think as an individual.

If your current existence is not what you envision for your life, you must embark on a personal (and individual) quest. An imperative quest, a necessary quest, a compulsory quest, this will be a quest that takes you to freedom; you alone must determine the course of your life direction.

As you wholeheartedly embrace your own freedom, so, too, must you also come to accept, to realize, to acknowledge, that *we are here to learn to live together amicably* even as others are willing (or not) to embrace the same.

In truth, as we work on our own growth, our own evolution, our own advancement, so, too, are we able to show others what is possible.

Friendship, cooperation, tolerance, understanding, empathy and compassion all have an enormous part to play in this quest that we seek.

Is not the quest to freedom also synonymous with the quest for a happy life, a peaceable life, a meaningful life?

What is Freedom?

Freedom is a word that means *a state of being free*.

Essentially, there are two types of freedom: [1] experiencing freedom *from something* and [2] having the freedom *to do something*.

———————◆✕◆———————

TYPE 1

Freedom from want means freedom from grave and extreme poverty that deprives one of the basic necessities of life (food, clothing, shelter, medical care, health).

Freedom from fear pertains to freedom from physical aggression (physical violence, domestic violence, verbal hostility, nonverbal intimidation, destruction of property, terrorism, warfare) which could possibly lead to anxiety, depression as well as other mental illnesses.

Freedom from adversity refers to freedom from an adverse (unfortunate) event or circumstance, often marked by misfortune, calamity or distress. While adversity (hardship) is said to be critical to growth and happiness, developing the attitude of seeing a misfortune as a blessing is imperative to the freedom process; *everything is a matter of perception.*

When you learn to accept the difficulties, the challenges, the lessons, interestingly enough, life becomes less burdensome, less troublesome, less arduous; in retrospect, the problem is not adversity, per sé, but both how you relate to it as well as what you glean from it.

Your reaction to any given circumstance can go one of two ways: you can either keep pouring fuel on the fire, to further fan the flames of discontent (anger, hatred, bitterness, revenge) or you can allow the fire to extinguish itself.

With a shift in one's thinking, one's perspective, one's approach, adversity can easily morph into opportunity; in this way, adversity is a most important teacher for each and every individual.

In the words of Frederick Douglass ...... *If there is no struggle, there is no progress. Those who profess to favor freedom, and yet depreciate agitation, are men who want crops without plowing up the ground. They want rain without thunder and lightning. They want the ocean without the awful roar of its many waters. This struggle may be a moral one; or it may be a physical one; or it may be both moral and physical; but it must be a struggle.*

Freedom from superstition relates to freedom from subversion (propaganda, deception, subterfuge, pretense, fraud, deceit, guile, cheating) on all societal levels (political, educational, religious).

Freedom from violence means freedom from the violent intention behind a thought (word or act) to do harm to another.

In its most positive form, the practitioner of ahimsa (non-violence) embraces love and forgiveness, applying the same rules to the wrong-doer, be they enemy, stranger, brother, father, son.

In the words of Mahatma Ghandi ...... *For me, non-violence is not a mere philosophical principle. It is the rule and the breath of my life. It is a matter not of the intellect but of the heart.*

So, too, did Mahatma Ghandi share ...... *One who hooks his fortunes to ahimsa, the law of love, daily lessens the circle of destruction, and to that extent promotes life and love; he who swears by ahimsa, the law of hate, daily widens the circle of destruction, and to that extent promotes death and hate.*

WE ALL MUST BECOME THE VERY CHANGE WE WISH TO SEE, WE WISH TO EXPERIENCE, WE WISH TO EXEMPLIFY, IN THIS WORLD.

Freedom from slavery pertains to freedom from slavery on all levels (emotional enslavement, mental enslavement, physical enslavement, debt bondage, forced prostitution, human trafficking).

Freedom from an un-chosen obligation refers to freedom from being made to act in violation of one's free, personal, individual, voluntary consent.

Freedom from oppression and persecution relates to freedom from cruel and unjust treatment (abuse of power, abusive relationships, ethnic cleansing, social inequality, socially supported mistreatment and exploitation, authoritarianism, humiliation, institutional oppression, resistance movements, political repression, police brutality, economic repression, racial segregation, totalitarianism).

Freedom from fear means freedom from a fear that serves to paralyze the individual to the degree that it stops them from doing something to achieve what it is that they want.

Freedom from fear of failure pertains to freedom from living such a cautious, and uneventful, life, that you will have never truly lived.

In the words of J. K. Rowling ...... *Some failure in life is inevitable. It is impossible to live without failing in something unless you live so cautiously that you might as well have never lived at all. In which case, you failed by default.*

Freedom from subordination refers to freedom from a life of servitude (submission, subservience, inferiority) to another.

Freedom from complacency relates to freedom from a life of comfort and security that results in a sense of smugness and superiority.

TYPE 2

Freedom of speech means having the freedom to be able to voice your thoughts, opinions and ideas publicly, without fear of censorship or punishment; herein, so, too, can one agree to disagree without fear of persecution.

Freedom of worship pertains to having the freedom to be able to practice whatever religion one chooses.

Freedom of conscience refers to having the freedom to change your religion or belief, without fear of censorship or punishment.

Freedom of movement relates to having the freedom to travel, reside in, and/or work in any part of a country (whilst still respecting the liberty and rights of others); such also allows one to leave any country, including his or her own, returning at any time.

Freedom of invention means having the freedom to create a product, or the introduction of a process, for the first time.

Freedom of initiative pertains to having the freedom to improve upon an existing product, process or service, whereby you are making a significant contribution.

Freedom of discovery refers to having the freedom to disclose relevant facts and documents in keeping with said discovery.

Freedom of equality relates to having the freedom to act towards one another in a spirit of brotherhood, knowing that all human beings are equal in dignity and rights.

Freedom of diversity means having the freedom to recognize, value and celebrate the different backgrounds, knowledge, skills, needs and experiences of each individual.

In so doing, we are able to make use of these differences (and individual strengths) to create a more cohesive and effective community which is able to provide for the full development of human potentiality.

It is within this frame of reference of an openness for differences, wherein it is safe to [1] express a contradictory opinion, [2] ask critical questions, [3] set aside prejudices and misconceptions, and [4] establish boundaries that enable you to decide how to live and work together, whilst respecting (and embracing) individual differences ...... that you can be who you are. Once you have been able to embrace, and set aside, the differences that abound, you are more apt to see (and focus upon) the shared similarities that flourish.

Freedom of time pertains to having the freedom to decide what you want to do with your time: taking the time to slow down and relax as often as you want, appreciating life in a much deeper way, having less routine and restrictions, displaying more flexibility to be spontaneous, spending your time engaged in remarkable, meaningful activity; in essence, it means living a more unconventional lifestyle.

Freedom of rationality (objective reality) relates to having the freedom to investigate and explore the unfiltered world that exists outside of our subjective (and biased) minds. The more we understand the view of objective reality, the more we know where we are in our own journey; likewise, the more we understand the view of objective reality, the more we know how distorted our subjective experience actually is.

Freedom of action means having the freedom to choose one set of circumstances or behaviors over another. Freedom of action is also about creating our environment and the world around us.

Freedom of thought and freedom of focus pertains to having the freedom to choose what we focus on, what we think, what we feel, how we feel. Knowing that our thoughts color our feelings, we are always free to choose freedom or bondage, happiness or unhappiness, euphoria or dysphoria, in each and every moment, despite the circumstances that exist.

You always have the *freedom to choose* **TO BE OR NOT TO BE**, as so eloquently put by William Shakespeare in the opening phrase of the soliloquy as pertains to the Nunnery Scene of Hamlet.

In truth, whilst happiness has nothing to do with how other people live their lives, it is about what you are able to do, for yourself; you are here to construct, to devise, to map out, a future that works for you.

The choice you make always leads to the road that you take.

The Imperative Quest To Freedom

Dr. Viktor Frankl, an Austrian neurologist and psychiatrist, as well as a Nazi concentration camp survivor, was of the belief that *choosing your attitude*, in any given set of circumstances, *is the highest level of freedom that exists.* [2] [3]

While there will be situations, feelings and experiences that serve to restrict you, to limit you, to confine you, such as [1] prejudice, [2] misconception, [3] fear, [4] rejection, [5] inability, [6] stress (workplace) [7] preconceived notions of what is possible, [8] preconceived notions of what is impossible, [9] ego, [10] impatience, [11] selfishness, and [12] procrastination, there will also be times when you have to work within the confines of the situation, the dilemma, the difficulty. If you were to immediately switch gears (thereby allowing for your given perception(s) and attitude(s) of the circumstance(s) to change), you might learn to refocus on having the freedom to do something valuable for yourself, something worthwhile for yourself, something appreciated by others.

---

[2] www.viktorfrankl.org
[3] https://www.brainpickings.org/2013/03/26/viktor-frankl-mans-search-for-meaning/

Changing your perception and choosing your attitude response can take you from the person that you are to the person that you can become, the person that you are meant to be.

Freedom in its most truthful and authentic state involves ......

DECIDING TO BE HAPPY RIGHT NOW IN SPITE OF ANXIETY, CHAOS OR DRAMA

FOCUSING ON GRATITUDE AND ABUNDANCE

ESTABLISHING HABITS, ROUTINES, GOALS THAT EMPOWER YOU AS AN INDIVIDUAL

In Search of Freedom

If the reality that you choose to experience is, indeed, built first in the mind, the first place that one must delve into is the belief system that one adheres to.

Life is all about living out your chosen beliefs.

A belief system is a strongly held opinion that determines how we perceive every aspect of our life by virtue of how we act, what we feel, what we think (which can often be judgmental) and how we form opinions.

You may consciously believe that you deserve to be highly successful, that you are capable of being highly successful; however, in spite of this conscious belief and your abilities, you do not succeed the way you believe you should. The reason you fall short of succeeding is based solely on a subconscious belief system that you cannot (or should not) succeed.

What we have programmed in our subconscious mind, from early childhood experiences, determines how we react today.

Regardless of what you think and believe consciously, it is *what you think and believe subconsciously* that *determines your life*.

How, then, do access our subconscious belief system?

How do we work to change our behavior patterns?

It is imperative to understand that belief systems are always meant to help at the time they are formed.

While they may end up creating disastrous results for the future adult (given their limiting and fear based entrapments), they are meant to help us get the love and attention we need, while also keeping us safe and protected.

The process of identifying your core belief system, your foundation, your nucleus, requires that you be completely honest with yourself.

While this is never an easy thing to do, it presents the opportunity to be more authentic.

Hypnosis is the most powerful tool available for accessing the subconscious mind. Through the use of hypnosis, you can quickly (and gently) get to the root cause of the problem (the issue, the life-long behavior patterns, the emotions, the habits); until a harmful belief is updated (through the acceptance of a more positive suggestion), you will continue to experience the disconnect between your conscious understanding and your controlling subconscious belief system.

One's belief system is actually two-fold in that [1] your beliefs determine who you are until such time as [2] you have learned to determine your beliefs for yourself.

Your belief system is what causes you to think.

Your belief system is what causes you to feel, to emote the emotions.

Your belief system controls the way you respond to situations, circumstances, individuals.

Until you learn to challenge, to re-think, to re-write, to re-configure, what you have long believed to be true, you take the beliefs that you hold as truth.

Until you learn to challenge, to re-think, to re-write, to re-configure, what you have long believed to be true, you take the beliefs that you hold as fact.

Until you learn to challenge, to re-think, to re-write, to re-configure, what you have long believed to be true, you take the beliefs that you hold as true as accurate.

As a result, you operate on automatic pilot, meaning that you do something (think something, say something, react to something) without thinking, simply because that is the way it has always been for you.

As long as you allow your belief system to unconsciously dictate what you do and experience, change is unlikely to find its way to your door.

As a result, you will continue to live a life based on the reality that has been created by the powers that have long hoarded the secrets, by the powers that have been in control of the plentiful disinformation (half-truths, deceptions and lies) and deliberate misinformation; in truth, theirs has always been an ingenious plan, and certainly one that a great many, including our parents and grandparents, have easily, and unknowingly, succumbed to.

As long as millions of people continue to focus their attention upon listening to the same words, seeing the same pictures and hearing the same message ...... all are unable to accept that they are powerful beings.

Most are completely unaware that their thoughts, their feelings, their desires, are the building blocks through which they can create their world.

This is the very truth that has been hidden from the multitude, cleverly disguised as the limiting beliefs that we have been conditioned to believe.

Limiting beliefs arise from a multitude of sources: past experience(s), the teachings of your parents, your families, your culture, social organizations, government agencies, religious organizations, educational institutions, political alliances; so, too, do limiting beliefs come from ourselves.

We have been conditioned to believe that ......

[1] everything that happens in life is due to random acts and circumstances (over which we have no control).

[2] one has to work hard to be successful; that nothing in life comes easily (we are pushed to work long hours, obey authority, seek job security, be loyal and conscientious employees).

[3] blind consumerism and materialism is the key to happiness (the more you have, the bigger you have, the happier you will be).

[4] normal human beings are monogamous (which merely serves to glorify the nuclear family while also stigmatizing many natural sexual desires).

[5] superficial social relationships, based mainly on appearances, as well as constantly comparing ourselves to others, and caring intensely what other people think of us (without any care to how we feel about ourselves), is important.

[6] we are entitled to what we want (immediate gratification; there is no waiting to be had, nor does self-regulation exist).

[7] we are entitled to blame others for our inadequacies, our faults, our incompetence.

[8] the absence of our own success is not our fault but the fault of the system (over which we have no control) because the rich always get richer and the poor always experience more poverty.

[9] showing emotion (of any kind) means that you are weak; being sensitive is considered a liability, even more so for males.

[10] the answer to everything we will ever need (and ever want) is to be found in the world of electronic devices (computers, iPads, internet, iPods, iPhones, Smartphones, video games, GPS, Bluetooth technology, webcams, Skype, digital cameras, 3D digital television).

[11] our religious belief is the true religion.

Unfortunately, this is the default pattern of thinking espoused by a great many.

Limiting beliefs are those that give one the illusion that they cannot do something, that they cannot be something, that they cannot have something or that something is not possible for them to achieve (and will never be).

Each time you use words *but, try, can't, someday, impossible, if, should, won't, maybe, quit* -- you are further limiting yourself. [4]

---

[4] https://www.tracibogan.com/personal-development/30-day-dreampreneur-challenge-delete-limiting-words/

Anything that limits (restricts, restrains, confines) can be referred to as a limiting belief.

Limiting beliefs hold you back from reaching your fullest potential.

As long as you accept, and practice, negative thinking as your habitual thought pattern, you believe yourself to be limited.

In addition, when you focus on the perception of lack and limitation, you merely attract more of the same.

The Ancient Greek aphorism *know thyself* is one of the Delphic maxims that was inscribed in the forecourt of the Temple of Apollo at Delphi, according to the Greek writer Pausanias.

For centuries, petitioners seeking advice from the oracle at Delphi would view the inscription.

Philosophers throughout the ages have continued to offer this same advice to their students; these words are as valuable today as they were almost three thousand years ago.

Part of knowing yourself is understanding your beliefs. The difficulty, however, is that most beliefs are subconscious, meaning that they have been accepted without ever having been critically examined.

The Search Continues

We are heavily influenced by our parents, family members, teachers, religious figures, media (television, newspapers, magazines, movies, internet), friends, acquaintances and propaganda (disinformation, indoctrination) ...... a condition that begins before birth and continues throughout childhood before advancing further into adulthood; so, too, are we influenced by life experiences and world events.

Like Pavlov's dog, we automatically learn to respond to environmental stimuli; a clear demonstration that we are programmed to think, feel, act and believe without conscious thought.

In the words of Dr. Maxwell Maltz ...... *Within you, right now, is the power to do things you never dreamed possible. This power becomes available to you just as soon as you change your beliefs.*

It is essential that you learn to see with your conscious (inner) eye as opposed to basing your beliefs on the outside world. As Marcel Proust has so astutely described, *the real voyage of discovery consists not in seeking new landscapes, but in having new eyes with which to see.*

In the words of Natalie Matoushek ...... *The real masters of consciousness, those living on the edge of thought, initiate their thoughts and beliefs based on inner reflection and the study of the universal laws. These masters see in their mind what they wish to believe; as a result, they actually see things into existence. A new reality can be created as one consciously alters their belief system. The reality we create, our outside world, is therefore dependent on our inside world. Our outside world is a mirror image of what beliefs, thoughts and feelings we hold in our minds. Life mirrors every aspect of us.* [5]

---

[5] Matoushek, Natalie. (2009) <u>What I Forgot The Day I Was Born</u> (page 64). Xlibris Corporation at www.Xlibrus.com

How people talk (their choice of words based on their view of the world) tells us a huge amount about what they think and believe in; often times, this is more important than the actual conversation taking place.

The Power of the Mind

While we openly acknowledge the mind to be incredibly powerful, we have forgotten that every feeling, every action, every obtained result, first began with a thought.

In fact, thought precedes everything; *all creation must first begin with a thought.*

As you expand your mind, as you exercise your mind, as you challenge your mindset (your paradigm), so that you may open up to the infinite possibilities that exist ...... you begin to summon your personal power.

Until you stop allowing yourself to be controlled by forces outside of yourself, you will never get to experience the astounding power of the mind.

In order to live a full life, a rewarding life, an exuberant life, a mindful life, an empowering life, an authentic life ...... you must learn to live from the inside out.

The mind is the connection that exists between the physical body and the spiritual body; as you come to strengthen the gap that exists between your conscious mind and your subconscious mind, so, too, are you strengthening your connection with Source.

As powerful as the conscious mind may be, the power associated with the subconscious mind is even more compelling in that the subconscious mind accepts whatever we tell it to believe; there is no perceived difference between right and wrong, real or imagined.

The real power of the mind lies at the subconscious level.

Our belief system is our view of the world, our perspective of reality.

It is our belief system that determines how we interpret the world, how we interpret our perspective of reality.

It is our belief system that serves to attract (or create) a life experience that serves to confirm what we believe.

If one is to alter this belief system, in order to eliminate limiting beliefs, conscious change must be addressed at the subconscious level of the mind.

Your beliefs are the hidden force that creates your reality. [6]

---

[6] https://trans4mind.com/counterpoint/index-happiness-wellbeing/ellerton2.shtml

Transformation in Action

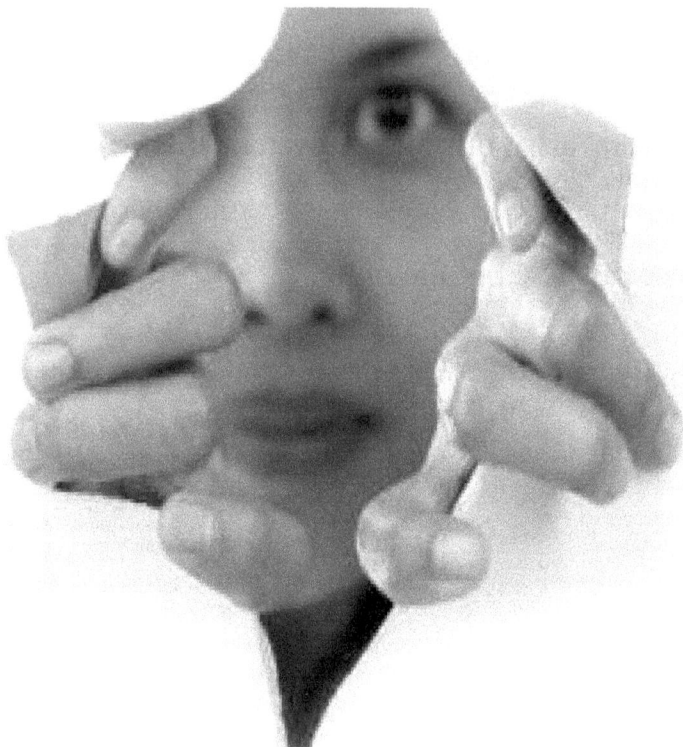

To become transformation in action, there are three key steps.

STEP 1 = IDENTIFYING BELIEFS

Core beliefs include *thoughts, assumptions and attitudes* that we hold about ourselves, about others, about the world around us.

Deep-seated beliefs, that constantly affect our lives, are referred to as core beliefs. They often go unrecognized; sometimes they are wrong.

Core beliefs affect what you achieve.

Core beliefs affect how you operate in the world.

As you can see, from the examples that follow, negative (and often inaccurate) core beliefs will drastically reduce one's chances at experiencing joy and self-fulfillment.

• I am ugly (plain, dull, undesirable, not lovable).

• I am not good enough (incompetent, not worthy, flawed, undeserving).

• I am unwanted (undesirable, defective, not special, a mistake).

• Everyone else is better at _____ than me.

• The world is full of selfish people.

• Everyone just wants to take; no one wants to give.

• I am powerless (helpless, weak, a failure, ineffective, a loser, inadequate).

• I am worthless (disposable, uninteresting, unimportant, a loser).

Often we are *completely unaware* of what are core beliefs are, even if we think we are conscious and awake.

The truth of the matter is that we all have core beliefs.

The truth of the matter is that we are all manipulated by them.

Core beliefs always start with "I .... "

Core beliefs are aptly named because they are *core* to your identity

So, too, are there supporting beliefs that uphold your core beliefs. For example, *she never really cared for me* supports the I am unlovable belief. In continuation, *he is such a show-off, it drives me mad* supports the I am unimportant, no one ever pays attention to me, belief.

Recording the thoughts you have about yourself (and other people) might be a good way to begin identifying these beliefs.

Next to each recorded thought, keeping asking the essential why questions until you arrive at a core belief answer.

You might write *I hate how my friend keeps interrupting me. Why is it so bad? Because I want to be listened to*. Why? *Because I want to be cared for*. Why? *Because I feel like no one cares about what I have to say*. Why is that so important? *Because I feel alone and worthless*. [7]

---

[7] https://lonerwolf.com/core-beliefs/

From this, one can ascertain the core belief to be either I am worthless or I am alone; perhaps both.

Beliefs are thoughts (over time) that we come to believe as true.

Beliefs are often developed based on our early experiences, which, for many people, do not reflect the truth; however, given that they feel so real, they can be very strong forces in shaping our perceptions. This is why they can be so difficult to change.

As has already been illustrated, it is possible to work towards identifying your core beliefs by starting with an automatic thought, after which you keep asking the pertinent questions until you reach the core belief.

Core Beliefs Inventory [8]

Core Beliefs Worksheet [9]

----

[8] https://www.thesantamonicatherapist.com/corebeliefs
[9] https://www.therapistaid.com/therapy-worksheet/core-beliefs

Identifying Core Beliefs Survey [10]

Self Defeating Beliefs Questionnaire [11]

The Core Belief Exercise [12]

There comes a time when many begin to question their beliefs, except for the ones they really believe. Ironically, those are the ones we never think to question (and very much need to).

Negative core beliefs are very much related to negative thinking tendencies in the present. They also play a major role in causing (and maintaining) various psychological issues that can often include depression, anxiety disorders, substance use disorders and eating disorders.

The best way to determine if you have negative core beliefs is to notice the prevalent themes in your thinking.

_____

[10] https://www.surveymonkey.com/r/FW_Core_Beliefs
[11] testandcalc.com/Self_Defeating_Beliefs/questtxt.asp
[12] susanshehata.com/wp-content/uploads/2014/06/The-Core-Belief-Exercise.pdf

If you tend to think in an absolutistic negative way about yourself, other people, or the world, it suggests that a core belief may be operating.

We know that core beliefs are associated with strong emotion; another sign that core beliefs may be present is the experiencing of strong emotional reactions in situations, particularly if the reaction appears out of proportion to events that are taking place.

Identifying Negative Core Beliefs [13]

Typical Negative Core Beliefs [14]

STEP 2 = IDENTIFYING (AND ELIMINATING) LIMITING BELIEFS

Limiting beliefs are the negative thoughts that you think over and over and over again. The more energy you give to these thoughts, the more you think about them.

---

[13] https://henrygrayson.com/wp-content/uploads/2014/04/Book-Identifying-Negative-Core-Beilefs-For-Clearing1.pdf
[14] www.core-beliefs-balance.com/example_negative_core_beliefs.htm

Unfortunately, *limiting beliefs are incredibly powerful* in that they serve to create the negative manifestations in your life, preventing you from creating what you want most.

Limiting beliefs tell you that something is impossible to do, to have, to be. In the astute words of Dr. Wayne Dyer: *the only limits we have are the limits we believe.*

Uncover Your Limitations Webinar [15]

Some people have successfully used EFT Tapping to eliminate (and flip) negative and limiting beliefs. [16] [17]

EFT (Emotional Freedom Technique) Tapping is a form of psychological acupressure, based on the same energy meridians used in traditional acupuncture to treat physical and emotional ailments for over five thousand years, but without the invasiveness of needles.

---

[15] https://www.youtube.com/watch?v=Vx52utPkhuQ
[16] www.practicalwellbeing.co.uk/wp-content/uploads/pw-flipping-beliefs-with-eft.pdf
[17] https://practicalwellbeing.co.uk/how-to-neutralise-limiting-beliefs-with-exception-tapping/

Learned in a matter of minutes, EFT Tapping can be used to apply instant relief to stressful situations in your life.

It was Aristotle who said ...... *We are what we repeatedly do. Excellence, then, is not an act, but a habit.*

As we know, habits are behavior patterns acquired by way of frequent repetition. They can be contributive, helpful and favorable; so, too, can they be harmful and hurtful, posing adverse affects.

Eliminating Limiting Beliefs [18]

Happiness Through Self-Awareness [19]

Letting Go Of Limiting Beliefs: Stepping Into Your Power [20]

The Importance of Examining Your Beliefs [21]

---

[18] zazenlife.com/2013/05/10/eliminating-limiting-beliefs/
[19] pathwaytohappiness.com
[20] https://www.youtube.com/watch?v=TX0hRPUmV7Y
[21] http://www.eruptingmind.com/the-importance-of-examining-your-beliefs/

The Peril of Limiting Beliefs [22]

The Power of Belief Systems: When You Change Belief Systems, You Change Your Life [23]

STEP 3 = REBOOTING THE SYSTEM

It was Gustave Flaubert who said .... *There is no truth; there is only perception.*

These words appropriately fit the fact that many of our beliefs (the thoughts we hold as true) are based solely on perception, as opposed to truth.

These words, then, lead one towards trying to identify that which is truth.

We base our perception (of ourselves and our surroundings) on the knowledge we have gathered over the years, quite oblivious to the fact that these beliefs might be false.

---

[22] https://gutsisthekey.com/2014/06/16/the-peril-of-limiting-beliefs/
[23] https://www.yourdailylifecoach.com/change-belief-systems.html

Our mindset consists of beliefs (which are thoughts that are repeated over and over for a period of time) that determine how we respond to situations.

The longer we think that something can or cannot happen, the more we believe that thought and the more we act accordingly.

I AM
two of the most
powerful words.
For what you put
after them
shapes your reality.

In order to reprogram our mind, we need to begin with perception (what you believe to be true about yourself and the world around you).

Beliefs are automatically instilled in us, courtesy of our family, friends, peers, teachers, culture, society, media.

Unless we are able to change these beliefs by overriding what we currently believe, then we always revert back to the default mode aspect of our brain.

The future is yours

Now you have two, conflicting beliefs about yourself: the auto-suggestion (conditioned) belief and the self-suggestion (liberated, empowered) belief (that you want to have about yourself and about your life).

This results in what is called cognitive dissonance; the state of having inconsistent thoughts, beliefs or attitudes, when you are needing (wanting) to focus on behavioral decisions and attitude change.

Assuming an empowering identity (reality) is always difficult in the beginning, but as you persist in living according to new belief system, you begin to create the frame of reference to back that belief up.

According to Maxwell Maltz, author of Psycho-Cybernetics, he shares that *the human nervous system cannot tell the difference between an actual experience and one imagined vividly and in detail.*

If you want to believe that you are more confident, more smart, more attractive, vividly imagine yourself acting and being exactly how you would want to be in each situation. In psychology, this is referred to as implosive therapy.

In essence, you keep persisting until your new (empowering) belief becomes your standard thought-pattern. Basically, you fake it until you make it (until you start believing in it).

With time being the gradual change agent between the two conflicting beliefs, persistence is key.

Over time, the new (empowering) belief will override (and eliminate) the old (disempowering) belief. When the new (empowering) belief becomes auto-suggested, or automatic, you no longer have to deal with the cognitive dissonance.

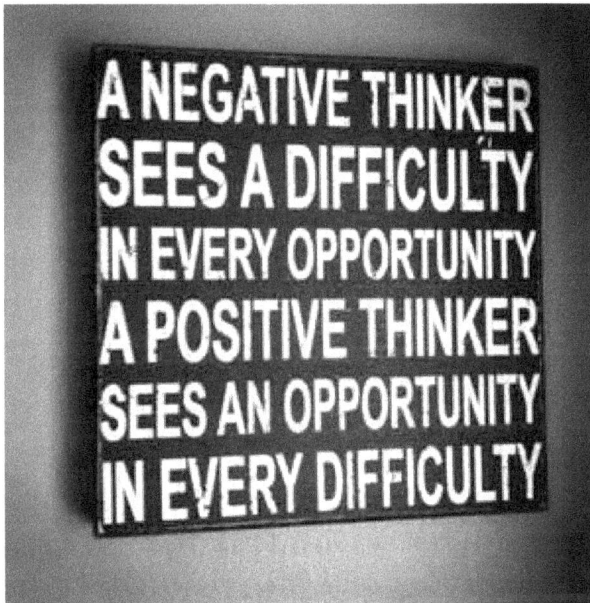

A NEGATIVE THINKER SEES A DIFFICULTY IN EVERY OPPORTUNITY A POSITIVE THINKER SEES AN OPPORTUNITY IN EVERY DIFFICULTY

You are what you think.

If you think negative, you will be negative.

If you repeat positive thoughts, your mind will begin to focus on what you want rather than on what you do not want.

You need to think positive, you need to think you can, you need to think above and beyond.

Unlearning everything you have learned, everything you have known, is the key to producing change that lasts.

Make a conscious effort to
surround yourself with
positive, nourishing, and

UPLIFTING PEOPLE—

people who believe in you,
encourage you to go after your dreams,
and applaud your victories.

— Jack Canfield

Simple Reminders
SIMPLEREMINDERS.COM

Surround yourself with positive people, with positive energy.

These are the people who are able to keep things in perspective. These are the people who do not readily jump to conclusions. These are the people who can help you see the opportunities within the change. These are the people who will be the ones who help you maintain high expectations.

Seek out those who are successful in doing what you need to do, or want to do, and use them as role models.

Align yourself with their way of thinking, with their mindset; allow yourself to be inspired.

The Positivity Virus [24]

You must believe yourself worthy of the new and empowered you. It is important to replace any self-limiting tape that your mindset might be playing with an updated one that contains the truth: you are worthy enough to have your goal, your dream, your desire, realized.

---

[24] zazenlife.com/2012/01/09/the-positivity-virus-2/

How To Destroy Limiting Beliefs and Reprogram Your Brain [25] [26]

How To Master Your Default Vibration [27]

How To Use Affirmations [28]

Lefkoe Method (TLM) [29]

Remove A Limiting Belief In 20 Minutes [30]

Reprogramming Your Subconscious Mind (Removing Negative Thought Patterns) [31]

---

[25] www.basicgrowth.com/reprogram-your-brain/
[26] https://www.youtube.com/watch?v=OMLTbYjrW4s
[27] zazenlife.com/2013/09/13/how-to-master-your-default-vibration/
[28] www.eatlivelife.com/2014/03/20/how-to-use-affirmations/
[29] www.mortylefkoe.com
[30] recreateyourlife.com/free/pavlina.php
[31] https://www.calmdownmind.com/programming-your-subconscious-mind/

Our Spiritual Side

When you seek the truth, it is important to know that the truth you identify is that which shall set you free from the ignorance that has long held you prisoner.

In having shared that humanity was created in the image of the Gods, so, too, does this mean that we were also given the power to create.

Each of us is currently creating and experiencing the contrast, the duality, the diversity, that this physical life offers; as a result, we are able to experience our spiritual selves in the fullest sense possible.

There are only two emotions; namely, love and fear.

These emotions serve to produce energetic vibrations that attract the very same into our lives, depending on that which we embrace.

Emotions related to fear (such as doubt, worry, envy, hate, pessimism, anxiety, despair, selfishness, betrayal, judgment) send forth low frequency vibrations.

Emotions related to love (such as happiness, joy, optimism, inspiration, confidence, calmness, reassurance, kindness, contentedness, altruism) send forth high frequency vibrations.

As long as fear-based thoughts dominate your thinking pattern, your paradigm, you will attract only fear-based events, people and circumstances into your life.

You have the power to consciously change negative thoughts to positive ones.

Feeling good is vital to living a happy, positive, empowered, mindful, authentic life.

Gratitude serves to keep you connected to living a happy, positive, empowered, mindful, authentic life.

The more that you have to be thankful for, the more you will be given to be thankful for.

In the words of Pierre Tielhard de Chardin ...... *We are not human beings having a spiritual experience; we are spiritual beings having a human experience.* To my way of thinking, this means that we are all connected, we are all of the same family. Truly, then, we have no need to compete, one against the other.

We are here to create individually, to co-create, to give of ourselves (our talents, our gifts, our passions) in service to each other, to embrace the Golden Rule (to honor and respect each other, to treat everyone with the utmost kindness, to refrain from making judgments against another), to appreciate the uniqueness and diversity of the experience.

As much as we are here to believe in ourselves, we are also here to learn to detach, emotionally, from the meaning that we assign to the situation, to the object, to the circumstance, to the event, so that we may become objective responders instead of subjective reactors.

In the words of James Allen ...... *Circumstance does not make the man; it reveals him to himself.*

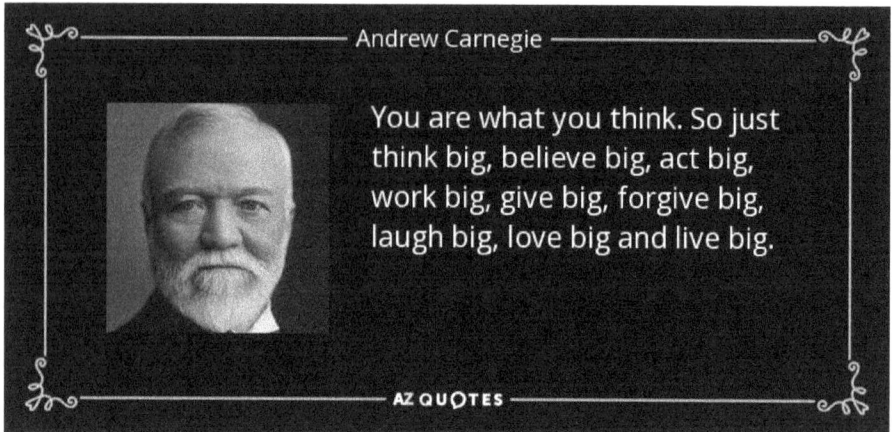

Andrew Carnegie

You are what you think. So just think big, believe big, act big, work big, give big, forgive big, laugh big, love big and live big.

AZ QUOTES

As Dr. Robert Schuller states ...... *You are what you think about all day long.*

Reclaim Your Dreams

We all want to live out our dreams, creating the life we want, but it can be intimidating, daunting and downright scary, especially when you are unsure what to do and where to start. With that in mind, now is the time to reclaim your personal power, your freedom, your authenticity. Playing it safe is not really a life; it is merely an existence.

To live life on your terms means taking ownership and responsibility.

To live life on your terms means becoming clear about what you want.

To live life on your terms means working hard to change your beliefs.

To live life on your terms means replacing old, ineffective, outdated and disempowering habits with more effective, empowering ones.

As you work to reclaim your dream, you begin to feel more vibrant, more alive, more fulfilled; so, too, will you discover that the most effective ways to improve your life usually go against conventional wisdom and societal expectations.

Even so, just imagine the positive impact you will have on this planet by having the courage to follow your dreams.

Paid to Exist: Live and Work on Your Own Terms [32]

Reclaim Your Dreams: An Uncommon Guide to Living on Your Own Terms (Jonathan Mead) [33]

The Courage To Live Consciously [34]

The Pursuit of Happiness [35]

---

[32] http://paidtoexist.com
[33] https://www.amazon.com/Reclaim-Your-Dreams-Uncommon-Living-ebook/dp/B007TXXZI0
[34] zazenlife.com/2012/01/08/the-courage-to-live-consciously/
[35] www.pursuit-of-happiness.org/history-of-happiness/viktor-frankl/

The Existential Question

Research continues to show that having purpose (passion) and meaning in life increases your overall well-being and life satisfaction, improves your mental and physical health, enhances your resiliency, enhances your self-esteem and decreases the chances of depression; in addition, the single-minded pursuit of happiness is actually leaving people less happy.

Ironically, it is the very pursuit of happiness, merely for the sake of said happiness, that serves to thwart happiness. [36]

The question, then, that bodes asking is this: do you see your life as meaningful (whole, satisfying, fulfilling) or meaningless?

---

[36] https://jezebel.com/5975308/you-might-be-happy-but-your-life-is-still-meaningless

Dr. Viktor Frankl

Dr. Viktor Frankl, a victim of the Nazi regime, spent several years in the Auschwitz concentration camp while his entire family, including both parents, passed away; whilst there, he deliberated on the meaning to be found in all of the death, suffering, and apparent meaninglessness, that was going on around him.

In his mémoire, entitled <u>Man's Search for Meaning</u>, he shares his conclusion ...... *Life is not primarily a quest for pleasure, as Freud believed, or a quest for power, as Alfred Adler taught, but a quest for meaning. The greatest task for any person is to find meaning in his or her own life.*

It becomes through purpose that you find passion, that you find happiness, that you find drive, that you find meaning in an apparently meaningless existence; so, too, does your passion also equate to your purpose.

The moment you identify your purpose (passion) becomes the very moment wherein you begin to feel more like a participant of your own life as opposed to the standoffish observer.

As Dr. Viktor Frankl continues to share ......

What matters, therefore, is not the meaning of life in general, but rather the specific meaning of a person's life at a given moment. To put the question in general terms would be comparable to the question posed to a chess champion: "Tell me, Master, what is the best move in the world?" There simply is no such thing as the best, or even a good, move apart from a particular situation in a game and the particular personality of one's opponent.

The same holds for human existence. One should not search for an abstract meaning of life. Everyone has his own specific vocation or mission in life to carry out a concrete assignment which demands fulfillment. Therein he cannot be replaced, nor can his life be repeated.

Whilst life is inherently meaningful, our lives can actually feel meaningless. This is a sobering thought, to be sure.

The only meanings that truly matter are the ones you have been able to work out for yourself, based on your own needs, your own desires, your own abilities, your own aptitudes.

When you take the time to use your own strength, your own sufficiency, your own wisdom, your own discernment, you will come to see that you are all that you need; you already have everything you need to figure out what your meaning is.

Your purpose in life can only be concluded by you.

As you find purpose in your life, you will inevitably inspire others. Everything you do, everything you say, everything you demonstrate, directly affects the people in your life at any given moment.

In the ever mindful words of Robin Sharma ...... *The purpose of life is a life of purpose.*

In the words of Nisargadatta Maharaj ...... *Wisdom is knowing I am nothing. Love is knowing I am everything. Between the two, my life moves.*

Leaders Who Show Zest For Life Help Mold Positive Outlook [37]

Man's Search For Meaning [38] [39]

Teacher's Guide: Man's Search For Meaning [40]

---

[37]
https://www.publicaffairs.af.mil/News/Commentaries/Display/Article/142230/leaders-who-show-zest-for-life-help-mold-positive-outlook/
[38] https://www.brainpickings.org/2013/03/26/viktor-frankl-mans-search-for-meaning/
[39] https://en.wikipedia.org/wiki/Man's_Search_for_Meaning
[40]
www.beacon.org/Assets/ClientPages/MansSearchForMeaningtg.aspx

The Paradox

The ultimate freedom is a paradox:
it is to experience yourself as a separate entity
connected with everything.

You cannot even imagine being inspired to fight for freedom, if you labor under the delusion that you are already free (as citizen-slaves of democracies do) or that you have an opportunity to obtain freedom by changing your form of government (as many citizen-slaves of communist, fascist, and totalitarian regimes believe). [41]

Freedom is an idea that someone is free, but is unable to be free. This is a form of an innate inability to act freely while having all the opportunities to do so; hence, freedom is a paradox. [42]

It was Thomas Hobbes who wrote ...... *if we are left to complete freedom without any restraints, we will fall prey to absolute chaos.*

Your own freedom is often used to limit the freedom of another person, meaning that to protect the other person, your freedom needs to be restricted, to be curtailed.

---

[41] https://forbiddentruthblog.com/2014/10/20/democracy-ultimate-freedom-illusion/

[42] https://prezi.com/-fsmih0z_zed/paradox-of-freedom/

In truth, democracies are said to be the greatest barrier to the enlightenment of the mind. Mayhap, then, the ultimate freedom can be likened to that of the physical death, even though energy cannot be destroyed.

As confusing as this may be, I am willing to equate ultimate freedom with my strength (and aptitude) to embrace the reality, to live the reality, to exude the reality, of my choosing, despite the chaotic collective experience that abounds.

The Forbidden Truth Blog [43]

Body, Mind, Spirit

Our world is made of body, mind and spirit; each of which has its own separate, and unique, function.

Causality is dually defined as [1] the relationship between cause and effect, and [2] the principle that everything has a cause.

In keeping with this definition, we can consider the body to be an effect that was created by a cause; namely, thought (mind).

Body cannot create; it can only experience and be experienced. Thought (mind) cannot experience; it can only create and interpret. As a result, thought (mind) needs a world of relativity (as in both the physical world as well as the physical body) to experience itself.

Spirit, on the other hand, is that which gives life to both thought (mind) and body.

The body, mind and spirit work together as a system of energy. This energy flow can be abundant or restricted, depending on our state of being in each moment; a state that changes constantly.

Our state of being is our overall feeling of health and wellness; a state that refers to how balanced we feel on all levels of our being.

Whether we are happy or sad, sick or well, disconnected from spirit or not, we are either in or out of alignment with who we really are.

Our thoughts, feelings, beliefs and attitudes can positively or negatively affect our biological functioning, meaning that our minds can actually affect how healthy our bodies are.

Likewise, extensive research is continuing to confirm the medical and mental benefits of meditation, mindfulness training, yoga and other similar mind-body practices.

When we are in alignment with who we really are, we experience joy in everything we do; so, too, do we treat others with love and respect as equally as we treat ourselves (and our bodies) with love and respect.

When we are out of alignment with who we really are, we experience the exact opposite.

When we are able to harmonise (balance) our state of being, we are in a better position to be able to create the life that we want.

[1] exercise regularly

[2] practice gratefulness, gratitude, appreciation

[3] get plenty of sleep (which serves to regenerate the body so that you can perform better the next day)

[4] breathe deeply

[5] practice different ways of grounding yourself and connecting to the frequencies of Mother Earth (spending time outside, walking barefoot on the earth, hugging a tree, replenishing your body with negative ions, employing the ancient technique of visualization)

Tree Meditation [44]

Mountain Meditation [45]

[6] eat organic produce

[7] drink clean filtered water

---

[44] www.wakingtimes.com/2013/09/21/8-methods-of-grounding-and-connecting-to-the-earths-frequencies/
[45] Ibid.

[8] embrace yoga (as well as tai chi) as a physical discipline

[9] smile often, engaging in heartfelt laugher (reduces the production of stress hormones)

[11] spend more time with those you love

[12] live a life of passion by doing more of what you love

[13] set time aside, each day, to rest your mind, courtesy of meditation

[14] embrace mindfulness and non-judgment as a lifelong discipline

[15] spend more time in nature

[16] eat dark, leafy greens that are rich in vitamins, minerals and chlorophyll (they help to alkalize and detoxify the body)

Here is a wonderfully illustrative story as per *The Mind, Body and Soul Connection* article by Larry Lewis [46] ......

A great Master once asked one of his students to pursue not only his academic studies but also his spiritual studies, so that he could learn the importance of improving his character and performing good endeavours.

The student replied that his diary was too full and he could not possibly do it.

---

[46] https://www.healthylifestylesliving.com/enlighten-the-soul/the-mind-body-and-soul-connection/

Then he looked at the Master and quickly comprehended that the Master's schedule was far busier than his own.

Realizing his dilemma, he asked the Master ......

How do you do it Master? How do you have the strength and stamina to work as hard as you do?

The Master replied ......

Every person has both a body and a soul. It is like a bird and its wings. Imagine if a bird were unaware that its wings enabled it to fly, they would only add an extra burden of weight. But once it flaps its wings, it lifts itself skyward. We all have wings -- our soul -- that can lift us as high as we need go. All we have to do is learn to use them.

Living in the Moment

When you take the time to free your mind, living in the moment, there will be times when you feel absolutely free.

This feeling has also been referenced as being in the Zone (something that Zen monks practice).

Today me will live in the moment, unless it's unpleasant, in which case me will eat a cookie.

• Cookie Monster

In the words of Lao Tzu ...... *If you are depressed, you are living in the past. If you are anxious, you are living in the future. If you are at peace, you are living in the present.*

Quantum Physics

In his book, <u>Quantum Consciousness</u>, Stephen Wolinsky shares that the entire universe is made up of energy in the form of a wave. In addition, subatomic particles (the tiniest particles we know about) are made up of wave energy. When these particles are observed, they individualize, meaning that they become a separate identity.

It was Sir Arthur Eddington, the famous English Physicist, who said that the universe in which we live *is a creation of our minds*.

It was Sir James Jeans, an equally famous personage of the same field, who suggested that the universe was merely *a creation that resulted from the thought of some great universal mind underlying and coordinating all of our minds*.

Interestingly enough, science has been uncovering parallels between the behavior of subatomic particles and various tenets of Eastern metaphysics. [47 48 49 50 51 52 53 54]

<hr />

The world of Quantum Physics states that nothing is solid.

Quantum Physics has proven that thoughts are what put together and hold together the ever-changing energy field into the so-called objects that we both see and touch. This means that everything we see in our physical world first started out as an idea, an idea that grew as it was shared and expressed.

[47] https://www.cfpf.org.uk/articles/rdp/caasqp/caasqp.html
[48] www.bizcharts.com/stoa_del_sol/plenum/plenum_3.html
[49] www.quantumconsciousness.org/content/overview-sh
[50] lightomega.org/Quantum-Physics-and-Evolving-Consciousness.html
[51] www.victorzammit.com/evidence/quantumphysicsdiscoveries.htm
[52] www.advaita.org.uk/extracts/science_wolfe.html
[53] www.hinduwisdom.info/articles_hinduism/287.htm
[54] https://witnessthis.wordpress.com/2011/05/09/a-dummies-guide-to-quantum-physics/

From a literal standpoint, *we become what we think about the most*; so, too, does our life become what we have imagined, and believed in, the most.

The outer world is literally our mirror, enabling all to experience in the physical plane that which they hold as their truth.

Throughout the universe, subatomic particles and atoms act as if they are connected; this is what we refer to as quantum entanglement.

Quantum entanglement means that "every action, thought, feeling and emotion is connected and can affect the whole in one manner or another." [55]

Made up of atoms, photons and electrons, we are always in a constant state of vibration.

---

[55] https://www.collective-evolution.com/2013/01/20/quantum-entanglement-what-it-is-and-why-its-relevant/

As a result, "our emotions, feelings, hearts and minds have the ability to affect what frequency our molecular structure vibrates at." [56]

Quantum entanglement is easily observed at a physical level, meaning what we do to one particle at one location, happens to another particle at a different location.

In keeping with the way you perceive reality, your consciousness is responsible "for the way your physicality acts and reacts to different experiences in your life. The energy you emanate, by frequency, is speaking to the universe and each other." [57]

Clearly, we are all connected, we are all one.

No matter what we do, think, say or feel, our actions have an effect on the world around us.

---

[56] https://www.collective-evolution.com/2013/01/20/quantum-entanglement-what-it-is-and-why-its-relevant/
[57] Ibid.

Every thought, every feeling, every emotion experienced, serves to keep energy in motion, creating and re-creating the world.

If we can interact with the energy around us, just by thinking about it, this means *our thoughts have the power to influence our reality*. In other words, we can shape our own reality just by thinking about something.

If your perception is that you simply cannot make your life any better, or that you really do not deserve to have the things you want, then *that* is the reality you are creating.

If, on the other hand, you think that everything happens in your life because you want it, then you will start to see changes taking place on a regular basis.

Clearly, one's perception plays an important role in how they see their life unfolding.

Everything is Energy

The entire universe is an energetic one.

Energy is how the universe communicates.

Energy is intelligent, pulsating, alive, caring, creative and ever changing (in form).

In order to draw that which you desire to yourself, your emotional energy (thoughts, feelings, tone) must be a congruent (corresponding, identical) vibrational match.

Mainstream media is biased and controlled; there is much disinformation and deliberate misinformation. If the news anchors can incite the same feelings (emotions) in millions of viewers, one has to ask where this energy goes?

I see this as comparable to the biggest source of psychic vampirism on a global level?

In taking time to push aside all distractions, belief systems, outmoded and outdated paradigms, disinformation as well as deliberate misinformation ...... the truth (the light) will appear.

I choose to accept my own power, to acknowledge my own power, to wield my own power.

I AM all-powerful.

Where do you choose to place your focus?

Remembrance

Living on this majestic planet, we are here to remember our natural state of totality; one of complete freedom, without limitation. [58] Once we come to accept this truth, this reality, we are able to release all of our preconceived limitations.

Whatever you look at, whatever you hear, whatever you sense, is through your mind. [59] As you change your mind (inner world), everything on the outside (outer world) changes as well.

When you change your thinking, you have fundamentally changed that aspect of your world that you have the power to change. The obstruction that must be eliminated (and completely obliterated) is the *illusion* of separation.

---

[58] www.stillnessspeaks.com/sitehtml/llevenson/keystoultimate.pdf (Session 1)
[59] Ibid.

We must use the mind to undo our perceived limitations, first turning the mind back upon the mind to discover what the mind is, and then going beyond the mind to experience the authentic Self, one of infiniteness, wholeness and total perfection. [60]

How, then, does one turn the mind back upon the mind in an effort to discover what the mind is?

Quite simply, you begin by looking at your mind.

As an objective observer, you begin to watch your thoughts; you simply become witness to your thoughts, without judgment, without fear of repercussion.

In order to re-discover the unlimited BEings that we are, we must quiet the mind, and finally let go of the mind, for this is the only way that it can be achieved.

---

[60] www.stillnessspeaks.com/sitehtml/llevenson/keystoultimate.pdf (Session 1)

The job that we must tackle is *the undoing of our negative thinking* so that we may begin to traverse in the right direction; after that, when all thinking, both negative and positive, ceases, we will find ourselves in the realm of knowingness, of omniscience, where there is no need to think because everything is known and all are joyous and totally free. [61]

Truth can never be found in the world; instead, we must journey within, for it is there that we will remember that I am you and you are me, that there is only one Mind, one Consciousness, despite the illusion of separation, as created by us.

While books, teachers, programs and many different transformational tools can point us in the right direction, as has been my personal exploration these past twenty+ years, in truth, it all comes down to the experiential, to the observed.

---

[61] www.stillnessspeaks.com/sitehtml/llevenson/keystoultimate.pdf
(Session 4)

Metaphysics

A Metaphysician is someone who is able to make changes in the physical world through meta-physical principles, meaning that they make use of the principles of mind (and beyond) to create powerful and lasting change in their own lives.

Within the metaphysical realm, man is creator; quite simply, this means that it is the thought (mind) that controls (creates) each individual reality, meaning that *if you think it, it is so*.

In living metaphysical principles, it is through the awareness of personal thoughts that every individual comes to discover that they are not a victim of circumstance. Instead, each comes to fully embrace, and acknowledge, that *life actually follows a pattern according to conscious, and subconscious, thoughts*. Becoming consciously aware of this thinking process, therefore, is a fundamental principle of metaphysics.

Parmenides, an early 5th century Greek philosopher, and founder of the Eleatic school of philosophy, was among the first to propose two differing views of reality (courtesy of a poem, entitled <u>On Nature</u>, his only known work that remains). The section called *the Way of Truth* discusses what is real, while the section called *the Way of Opinion* discusses that which is illusionary.

There are many twenty-first century comparisons that we can draw between these fifth century words, especially as Parmenides shares that there are but two methods of inquiry; namely, that which is and that which is not. Heavily debated since his time, these words have been taken to mean that existence is timeless and eternal, indestructible and unchanging, whereas it becomes in the world of appearances that one's sensory faculties generally lead to conceptions that are both false and deceitful. In summation, truth cannot be known through sensory perception for the simple reason that the perception (appearance) of things is deceptive. What exists, therefore, must always exist; this is what Parmenides is saying. On the other hand, and from a paradoxical standpoint, if you will, perception is important.

We view the world from our own internal frame of reference (based on beliefs and previous associations stored in the brain), which is why everyone experiences situations in their own unique way. Perception, then, can be defined as an image of reality that our brain constructs from that which is known.

There exists a secret in this vast universe of ours: if you can change the way you perceive any given situation, then each context, thereafter, will have changed. In essence, *if you can change the way you look at things, the things you look at will change.*

It is metaphysical mind that demonstrates the ability to heal the body, to create or deny peace, and to bring one into conscious awareness; the very same beliefs as held true by Jesus. In reference to the principles of cause and effect, it is known that for every action, there is an equal, and opposite, reaction; likewise, for every force there is an equal, and opposite force. Following the same train of thought, this simply means that like attracts like.

According to the Law of Attraction, we attract into our lives that which we think about. If you are thinking about something because you *want* it, you have attracted that very thought into your life. If you are thinking about something because you *do not* want it, you have also attracted that very thought into your life.

Once you think a thought, you are bringing that thought into physical existence. You can think about material things. You can think about particular events or circumstances. You can think about feelings and emotions. In truth, the universe does not care what we think about or why we think about the things that we do; the universe simply responds to our thoughts, bringing us what we are thinking about.

This is where focus thought and determination becomes extremely important, in that you need to know *what you want* as well as *what you do not want.* If you continue to focus on good things, then good things shall come to you.

When René Descartes wrote *I think therefore I am* (Cogito ergo sum) in the 17th century, he was proclaiming the importance of our thought processes.

Emotions help us attach significance, importance and understanding to the things we experience in our lives. As a matter of fact, one of the most powerful driving forces in our lives is the pursuit of happiness.

Emotions give substance to our thoughts; hence, herein lies the secret; if you can ……

[1] remain focused on what you want

[2] imbue that desire with the *strongest* emotion you can think of

[3] spend your time relaxing, acting only when you feel inspired to do so

…… you will be able to attract, into your life, that which has become your intention (your focus).

Thoughts are energy; energy is what reality is made of. Each time you think a thought, you are changing the energy field of the reality that surrounds you. Learning to reverse mental negativity is absolutely crucial to your health and well-being on all levels (physical, mental, emotional spiritual).

Witness to Your Thoughts

William Shakespeare

There is nothing either good or bad, but thinking makes it so.

———————◆◈◆———————

We are living in a time where everything may seem hopeless, where everything feels hopeless.

The moment we utter the words *I have a problem*, we have made it real. Even in uttering the words *there is no problem*, we are still mentally holding onto the problem, sustaining it even further.

The 2012 to 2013 school year was evidence of my low spirits and dashed hopes because I ended up creating a teaching assignment situation that I did not want, simply because I was holding onto the so-called problem.

Anytime we experience what we perceive to be a problem, we are operating (reacting) as limited ego and whenever you attempt to express the authentic Self through the limited ego (which is much too small), we get squeezed and it hurts. [62]

While I understood what I had to do from an intellectual standpoint, it appeared that I still had an important lesson to learn in becoming a detached observer to the thoughts that continued to invade my physical being.

We are here to realize that this is a mental world, a world of our own creation; so, too, are we here to realize that we are not this body, not this mind, not this world. This knowledge, this reality, this truth, is what enables me to reflect back on past experiences, heart based consciousness experiences, whereby everything seemed to fall into place perfectly, harmoniously, and with very little effort, for these were the times when I was expressing as authentic Self.

---

[62] www.stillnessspeaks.com/sitehtml/llevenson/keystoultimate.pdf (Session 2)

Even limited ego creations serve as an experience that can be learned from; a blessing in disguise, if you will. The more "ego motivated we are, the more difficult it is to accomplish something, the less harmony there is and the greater the misery we have." [63]

In fact, when people are saying things about you, opposing you, this can be taken as a good opportunity to grow because it gives you a chance to practice the real Love, the real Peace. [64] In this way, opposition can be seen as a very healthy thing.

---

[63] www.stillnessspeaks.com/sitehtml/llevenson/keystoultimate.pdf (Session 2)
[64] www.stillnessspeaks.com/sitehtml/llevenson/keystoultimate.pdf (Session 3)

We can strive to become that detached and objective observer by eliminating all negative words from our vocabulary; words like *problem, can't, don't, won't, hate, impossible, fed up* and *invalidated*, to cite a key few. [65]

We need to stop thinking, speaking and writing negative words, replacing them with positive. People *simply do not realize the full impact* that negative words have on their subconscious mind.

As an empath, I find it extremely challenging to deflect negativity when one's place of work is profoundly affected; it eventually seeps directly into your pores, but not without having made countless attempts (by way of affirmations, mantras, and the carrying of specific crystals and stones) to avert the aura intruder.

It appeared that I still had an important lesson to learn in this department as well.

---

[65] eqi.org/fw_neg.htm

In becoming witness to our thoughts, so, too, does this allow for subconscious thoughts, many of which are ego-driven, to come to the fore of the conscious mind; accept them, without attaching any emotional response to them, and then allow for their release.

Visualize them floating away on the wind. Karma is in "the thought, not in the act. When you learn to eliminate subconscious thought, you also eliminate future karma, mainly because it is the thought that carries over from lifetime to lifetime." [66] Everything we see in the world, we see only in our mind. Nothing can be seen "except through our consciousness. Whatever we see is in our consciousness, in our mind. When one begins to realize this, then one works to change one's consciousness and by so doing, one changes his environment." [67]

---

[66] www.stillnessspeaks.com/sitehtml/llevenson/keystoultimate.pdf (Session 16)
[67] www.stillnessspeaks.com/sitehtml/llevenson/keystoultimate.pdf (Session 4)

Eventually you will find yourself simply watching your own body, knowing that it is not you, knowing that neither are you limited, or bound, by it.

This is when you are finally free to use your physical vehicle (the body) to help others evolve, for you will have arrived at the ultimate truth; that you are the world. You are the universe, loving everyone, unconditionally, that has chosen to be here, participating, with you.

When you fully love someone, becoming one with them, you exude the grand and glorious infinite BEing that you are.

Realization

Most of us already have the intellectual knowledge and yet are not realized; what we are striving for is knowledge through experience, through feeling, through inner sight, through realization, through integration. [68]

As one contemplates this knowledge, it has to resonate, meaning that it has to feel right. When this happens, the knowledge has become a revelation, an AHA moment, something that you are really seeing for the first time, even though you may have heard it again and again and again. This internalized revelation, then, is considered to be non-intellectual, even though the means through which it is attained is primarily intellectual in nature. Simply put, we use the mind to direct the mind toward the answer; an answer that comes from the realm of knowingness, the realm of omniscience.

---

[68] www.stillnessspeaks.com/sitehtml/llevenson/keystoultimate.pdf (Session 6)

By quieting the mind through the stilling of your thoughts, everyone has access to this realm; the state where you greet your authentic, infinite, perfect, and unlimited, Self. There is also an interesting paradox associated with thought in that *the conscious thought is only the unconscious thought made conscious.* [69]

Only in the waking state can we release these thoughts, eliminating them from our lives, so that we are better able to access the super-conscious realm; that which is all awareness and all knowingness, for there is no thinking when you know. [70]

Thoughts *are* things, so it is imperative you learn to master your mind.

Thoughts direct action; thoughts have power. So, too, does this mean that you must create the state from which you live. As consciousness, you have the power to set yourself free.

---

[69] www.stillnessspeaks.com/sitehtml/llevenson/keystoultimate.pdf (Session 6)
[70] Ibid.

We create our lives through our own thought processes.

What you say creates what you believe. What you believe impacts how you behave. What you believe impacts the choices you make. What you believe impacts the way your life will be. You are the legacy that you leave behind.

In the words of Dr. Amit Goswami, Theoretical Nuclear Physicist, University of Oregon Institute of Theoretical Science ... *If ordinary people really knew that consciousness, and not matter, is the link that connects us with each other and the world, then their views about war and peace, environmental pollution, social justice, religious values and all other human endeavors would change radically.*

In the words of Marcus Aurelius .... *When you arise in the morning think of what a privilege it is to be alive: to breathe, to think, to enjoy, to love.*

Responsibility

I am responsible for everything that I think, for they are my thoughts. As soon as I take responsibility for my thoughts, I am in control. I can turn them off, I can reverse them, I can neutralize them, I can change them, I can overcome them.

I am responsible for everything that I say, for they are my words.

I am responsible for everything that I feel, for they are my emotions. I choose to feel angry. I choose to feel hurt. I choose to feel miserable. I choose to feel happy.

I am responsible for everything that I do, for they are my actions.

I am responsible for everything that I do not do, for they are my inactions.

Knowing that I am the creator of my life, the next meditative thought becomes: *what is it that I wish to create?*

So, too, is this the place whereby one must become *very careful* about what they wish for.

On the flip side of the responsibility coin lies another important assignment. We are not obligated to help those who do not want our help, for that would be an imposition. Those that want our help will find us.

Once we have learned how to better control our own lives, making ourselves happier as a result, we are able to focus on making life happier for others.

As we begin to live more expansively, thinking less about ourselves and more about others, demonstrating an attitude of love as well as a feeling of compassion and oneness with everyone, this is when we *really* begin to help ourselves.

Love is only understood when you love.

Compassion means understanding what others are experiencing.

The Magic of Believing

Claude M. Bristol, The Magic of Believing

No mind ever receives the truth until it is prepared to receive it.

***

Belief is the motivating force that enables you to achieve your goal.

It is vital that you know *exactly* what you desire.

What is your goal? Have you visualized what you *really* want? If wealth, can you fix the amount in figures? If achievement, can you definitively specify what you want to achieve?

Thoughts become real when we affix our imagination steadily upon them.

We know that fearful thoughts become just as creative and magnetic as constructive and positive thoughts.

Claude Bristol believed there to be a corresponding factor between one's thoughts along with their pitch, intensity, emotional quality, depth of feeling and vibratory plane.

This means that thoughts can either be [1] creative or [2] controlling.

When a thought is completely rounded out, meaning that you have visualized the fulfillment of your desire and are able to see, in your mind, a picture of the object you desire (as if you were already in possession of it), this is when it carries the much needed impetus.

The conscious mind is the source of thought.

The chief powers of the conscious mind involve reasoning (inductive, deductive, analytic, synthetic), logic, judgment, calculation and rationalization, wherein we observe through the five senses.

The subconscious mind, on the other hand, is the source of power.

The chief powers of the subconscious mind involve intuition, emotion, belief, conviction, assuredness, inspiration, imagination, suggestion, organization and memory, operating most successfully when the perceived five senses are inactive.

Interestingly, it was Theodore Simon Jouffroy, the French philosopher, who stated that *the subconscious mind will not take the trouble to work for those who do not believe in it.*

———————————❖———————————

A Biography of Claude M. Bristol [71]

_____

[71] claudebristol.wwwhubs.com

Living in the Now

Living in the NOW means gives you the opportunity to focus your energy on DOING.

Living in the NOW means that your time and energy is no longer fragmented.

Living in the NOW means experiencing yourself as a whole person.

Living in the NOW means being fully committed to your present goals and ambitions.

Living in the NOW means that you are not thinking about the past.

Living in the NOW means you are not worried about the future.

Living in the NOW enables you to focus on new beginnings.

Conviction

The power of suggestion, by way of repetition (of the same chant, the same mantra, the same incantations, the same affirmations), is what leads to belief. Once the belief becomes a deep conviction, things begin to happen.

Suggestion can be [1] auto-suggestive (the suggestion comes from you) or [2] hetero-suggestive (the suggestion comes to you from outside sources). So, too, is suggestion the basic principle behind all successful advertising.

Repeated suggestion, delivered by the conscious mind, accompanied with a mental picture of the desired goal, thereby arousing the emotions, is what sparks the subconscious mind into action (manifestation).

Clearly, imagination, visualization (a clear mental picture) and concentration are the key factors needed to develop the magnetic forces of the subconscious mind.

Positive creative thought leads to action, but the real power, more than the action, is the thought.

It was Socrates who said *Know Thyself*, an aphorism that means when you know yourself, [1] you are willing to take the time to examine your core values (you know what you want and you know what you can do), [2] you are able to learn from your past so that you can make empowering choices, [3] you are able to live a life based on living your truth, and [4] you are open to change.

The more you know yourself, the more control (power) you will have in your life.

When you have the conviction that God is All, that God is Perfect, everything *must* be perfect, thereby leaving no place for imperfection or troubles. [72]

---

[72] www.stillnessspeaks.com/sitehtml/llevenson/keystoultimate.pdf (Session 2)

This is where *Letting Go in order to Let Happen* comes into play. I simply have to move my physical body out of the way, by letting go of the limited ego and becoming the witness, in order to enable that which is unlimited (God).

It takes more effort "to be limited when your natural state is unlimited." [73]

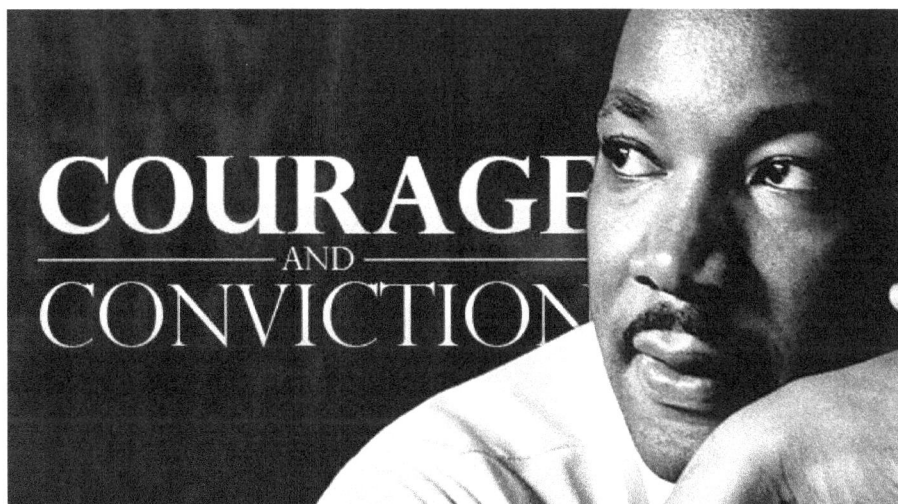

---

[73] www.stillnessspeaks.com/sitehtml/llevenson/keystoultimate.pdf (Session 2)

Manifesting

There is a difference between visualizing and manifesting.

There are several ways in which to visualize; namely, [1] internalizing (seeing the images in your mind's eye), [2] externalizing (projecting an image outside of your physical body, as in a vision board or a Mind Movie, which I have engaged in), [3] forecasting (seeing yourself at an imagined event), [4] emotionalizing (feeling the emotion and energy, but not actually seeing anything; which is my way of visualization) and [5] verbalizing (describing objects or events).

Visualization involves becoming focused on creating an *image* of a perceived reality, somewhere in the future.

Manifesting, on the other hand, is focused on creating the desired reality, in the here and now, wherein all your power and energy comes from the present, from BEing in sync with the cosmos. It is here that you set your intention and you fully expect that your desire shall be realized.

Be definite about what you want and do not change your mind. You must remain confident in your decision, allowing the universe to bring it to you. This first step is crucial.

It is important that your intention be clear, positive and specific; it is also important that it be worded in the present tense.

Pick one thing, remaining focused until it manifests for you, otherwise you might end up frustrated and confused, telling the universe that some things are more important than others. You might even end up railroading all of your good intentions, as has been the personal experience of a great many, myself included.

Instead of saying *I do not want to be doing this job anymore* (which is actually what I was doing, so, you see, there was much that I still needed to learn) reword it to something like *I want a job whereby I am a fully supported team player*.

There are times when it can be difficult to remain positive, but in the case of manifestation, this factor is an essential one.

As already indicated in the Metaphysics chapter, belief and perception work together. Thoughts that you think over and over again are what we call beliefs. When you change your beliefs, your perception also changes.

Knowing that thoughts are energy and that thoughts have power, you need to ensure that you are using your thoughts in a positive way.

Keeping your goal in mind, you must also trust that the universe shall deliver your desire to you.

The more excited we feel about having something, the faster our expectations are realized. This is why we need to keep taking the time to *reflect on how attaining this goal will make us feel*.

Emotions provide the much needed nutrients (akin to both sunshine and water) to the thought that has been planted.

Whenever you feel motivated by your impulses (intuition) to take action, do so; otherwise, just relax and go with the flow.

You must trust that the universe knows what you want and is endeavoring to bring it to fruition.

If you both know and believe that your desire will manifest, it is time to let the cosmos do what it does best.

Having the faith to *Let Go and Let Happen*, while remaining positive, is often the most difficult part.

This is where you are able to take the time to calm the mind, easing the worries and stresses of the day, thinking only about yourself and what you need to unwind.

When one keeps their mind filled with positive, powerful and creative thoughts, in truth, there is very little room, if indeed, any at all, for negative thoughts and doubts.

Be sure to express your gratitude.

Amit Goswami, The Self-Aware Universe

... every time we observe, there is a new beginning, then the world is creative at the base level.

Love

Thought is far more powerful than action, for it is the initiator that comes before and determines action.

Consciousness determines everything, the world being but the collective consciousness. If we do not like what is happening (in our outer world), all we need to do is change our consciousness (our inner world) and the outer physical world changes accordingly.

Becoming indifferent to the negativity that abounds is a most powerful place to be. The more you are capable of loving, the more you are helping. In bettering yourself, so, too, are you bettering the world.

Mahatma Gandhi was an incredible example of the power that exists in love. Teaching non-violence, he was able to win a war against Britain, without the use of force.

When we are emulating love, we are living as our God selves.

Love should be felt equally for all.

Love exemplifies giving; when things are given with this attitude, it is love.

The greatest gifts we can give, in love, are the gifts of wisdom and understanding.

Karma

Karma is a Sanskrit term that references action (deed). As such, it can be used to express the scientific law of cause and effect (which, according to Metaphysicians, is also one of the laws of the universe), meaning that *every action must have a reaction.*

Energy, as a force, consists of both positive and negative components, each of which acts upon the other to cause a vibration. Without these two opposing forces, there would be no life.

What this essentially means is that the totality of life acts (cause) and reacts (effect) because of this pull.

As you and I create our reality from these two forces, we do our best to try and reach a balance within each lifetime; this shows us how the life principle law of sowing (the seed) and reaping (the harvest) becomes both a scientific and spiritual law, called Karma.

When we think, speak or act, we initiate a force that will react accordingly

While negative karma can weigh down your soul, thereby hampering your personal evolution, the law of cause and effect is not one of punishment; instead, it is one that is necessary to our education, our learning, our wisdom, in that we are unable to escape the consequences of our thoughts (words, actions).

Whatever one directs outward (into the universe) always comes back; some refer to this as the Great Law.

If we want to reap the benefits of happiness, peace, love and friendship, so, too, must we BE happy, BE peaceful, BE loving, BE a true friend.

Those of us on the spiritual path know that life is not simply what happens to us, but is what is created by us, meaning that life requires our participation.

One's inner state dictates that which they are surrounded by.

When the body is at *ease* (as in mental, emotional, and spiritual harmony), so, too, is it healthy.

By comparison, when the body is at *dis-ease* (meaning mental, emotional, and spiritual disharmony), illness follows.

———————————◆✕◆———————————

One cannot change what one refuses to see, what one refuses to accept. If your version of reality is negative,[74] you have likely been conditioned to believe that whatever can go wrong, will go wrong and whatever can go right, will probably go wrong, too. These unconsciously held beliefs make you a negative person, even without your awareness.

The moment that you learn to express gratitude for what is (including the unpleasant lessons), you begin to invite more positive energy into your life.

———————————————

[74] https://in5d.com/how-negative-energy-affects-your-life-and-how-to-clear-it/

In order to grow (evolve, advance) as a person, you must be willing to embrace change, to become the change you wish to see in the world. It is true that we mirror what surrounds us. It is also true that what surrounds us is reflected back to us. This means that you must be willing to take ownership and responsibility for what is in your life, for what you want (need) to change.

Karma is "initiated in thought. Thought is the cause and action is the effect." [75]

Desire is what initiates the cycle.

Desire = Thought = Action

If the action does not fulfill the desire, we increase the desire and action; hence, the cycle.

---

[75] www.stillnessspeaks.com/sitehtml/llevenson/keystoultimate.pdf (Session 28)

When you have become witness to your thoughts, you are able to witness the duality that exists; an experience that is most conducive to spiritual growth.

From the highest vantage point that exists, when you are fully realized, you will look at the world, seeing only a singular Oneness, for all is your very own Self.

When you are able to see (experience) who and what you are, karma ceases to exist because there is only BEingness.

Happiness is our very own Self.

Happiness is our basic nature.

We do not need anything external to be happy.

The more you see (experience) who and what you are, the less you desire.

Every negative thought we have, whether we carry out the act or not, creates karma.

Karma comes to an end when "one recognizes that it is all in his mind and he is not his mind." [76]

The truest freedom lies in deciding "whether or not to identify with the body and its action(s). If an actor plays the part of a king or a beggar, he is unaffected by it because he knows he is not that character." [77]

It becomes in carrying out our part in the world, in this same manner, that we realize our true nature: that we are a grand and glorious BEing, our very own infinite Self.

---

[76] www.stillnessspeaks.com/sitehtml/llevenson/keystoultimate.pdf (Session 28)
[77] Ibid.

Total Mastery

A master is one "who is master over all matter in the universe, and who is master over his mind. A master is one who sees his own infinity within. A master is one who has undone all thoughts of limitation, who has ripped off all these sheaths of limitations, and is free." [78]

While I know, and believe, myself to be an unlimited BEing, I am far from being a Master. The way to this inner BEing is to direct our attention inward. We first focus the mind "back upon the mind until we discover what mind is (which is a limiting adjunct covering our unlimited BEingness). We then focus attention on our Self to discover our real nature." [79]

---

[78] www.stillnessspeaks.com/sitehtml/llevenson/keystoultimate.pdf (Session 7)
[79] www.stillnessspeaks.com/sitehtml/llevenson/keystoultimate.pdf (Session 9)

The prime obstacle that we meet is the subconscious mind.

All subconscious thoughts, as limiting as they are, keep directing us, sometimes even lifetimes, until we finally succeed in overcoming them. We are actually able to overcome them "with thoughts of what we *really* want to do in life, and in that way become matter over the mind, controlling the thoughts until only the thoughts we want determine our behavior." [80] This is when we find ourselves in the position of beginning to transcend the mind.

As we delve within, seeking and meditating to still the mind enough so to realize (experience) the infinite BEing that we are, this is where we begin to understand the truth of the matter; namely, that "we are master over matter (and matter includes the body)," [81] after which we also become aware that we are also master over mind.

---

[80] www.stillnessspeaks.com/sitehtml/llevenson/keystoultimate.pdf (Session 9)
[81] Ibid.

It is imperative, however, that you start with the first step, which is to *consciously* control matter.

Whether aware of it or not, everyone is controlling matter all the time. It is impossible not to be a creator all the time. As long as we are sporting a mind and a body, so, too, shall we be a creator.

We create with our thoughts, our feelings, our emotions, our actions, even our inactions; however, many are not aware of this fact.

This means that every single thought, materializes in the physical world. Every unconscious thought is active, as well, whether we are aware of it or not.

If we think the opposite, with equal strength, immediately after having had a thought, we can neutralize the thought. However, any thought that has not been reversed, or neutralized, will materialize in the future, if not immediately.

What we need to learn to do *consciously* direct our focus.

It becomes imperative that you learn to concentrate the thought (the focus) in the direction that you want, until such time as those thoughts become dominant over the subconscious thoughts.

Even if you find yourself unable to retrieve the subconscious thoughts that may be derailing your creation, it is possible to plant a conscious thought, placing incredible power behind it, so that it will override all prior unconscious thoughts. This is what we call using will power.

When you are feeling exuberant (energetic, enthusiastic, effervescent, elated, excited, exhilarated, high spirited, lively, passionate, sparkling, vigorous, vivacious), that is when you have the *greatest strength* to will that which you want.

The material world, big or small, is just an outward projection (a mental image, a mental picture) of our minds.

To get beyond creation, however, we must go beyond the mind.

This is a difficult concept for the mind to comprehend, primarily because the mind is constantly involved in creating.

The mind, as I have alluded to before, in earlier works, is the creating mechanism of the universe and yet the mind will never know God until you go above the mind. [82]

After you are able to master matter by consciously creating that which you want, which means that you have also stopped creating the things that you do not want, this becomes the time to master your mind and advance far beyond it.

---

[82] www.stillnessspeaks.com/sitehtml/llevenson/keystoultimate.pdf (Session 9)

Meditation

Most believe that to meditate means to quiet the mind and simply remain within that quiet space; a space that gives one a calm and relaxed feeling, but no knowledge.

Lester Levenson talks about Meditation from a different standpoint, believing the best type is one whereby you are armed with questions of personal significance, and you remain quiet until the answer shows itself. After that, you simply move to the next question of importance, doing the same.

Questions worth positing are:

[1] What is happiness?

[2] What is life?

[3] What do I want?

[4] How do I get happiness?

[5] What is intelligence?

[6] What is responsibility?

[7] What am I?

[8] What is this world?

[9] What is my relationship to it?

[10] What is holding me up?

As Lester shares, "the starting point *should be* a strong desire for the answer; when that desire is strong, we get the answer." [83]

Do not believe something simply because you have found it written in books of great import.

Do not believe something simply because it has been shared from a reliable source.

---

[83] www.stillnessspeaks.com/sitehtml/llevenson/keystoultimate.pdf (Session 11)

Do not believe something simply because it has been written by myself.

Do not believe in something simply because your elders deem it to be true.

You are here to experience, to prove this knowledge to yourself.

Meditation, according to Lester, should never be a passive endeavour where we try to force the mind to go blank.

As you enter into your Meditation, there are several centers you may concentrate on. Located between the eyebrows is the center for the Third Eye (the astral eye, the spiritual eye). When you focus on this area, you are pulled away from the lower centers (chakras) of the body. Some prefer the heart center as their point of focus. The heart is a good place because it is the center of feeling, and feeling is closer to the authentic Self than thought.

Regardless of the center you choose to focus on, concentrate on seeking the answer, for the answer becomes your quest.

Knowing that I have never been successful in trying to force my mind to go blank, maybe I ought to give this meditative version a try.

In the words of Andrew Cohen ...... *As I see it, the purpose of mystical experience is to convince us, at a soul level, that our true nature is Spirit—to convince us so deeply that we are liberated from existential doubt. Why? So we will finally be* available *to participate, consciously and wholeheartedly, in the greatest gift we've been given ... which is the life we are* already *living right now.*

In The Independent Mind: Learning to Live a Life of Freedom, Osho shares that our minds are running on malware programs; as a result, he introduces meditation as an antivirus to clean our minds of the conditionings and indoctrinations that are preventing us from realizing our full potential (which also includes being happy). [84]

---

[84] https://www.amazon.com/Independent-Mind-Learning-Live-Freedom/dp/1938755790/

Clearly, our minds have been hacked and may be infected.

Movement

Andrew Cohen

What gives me the greatest spiritual confidence is the knowledge that I'm moving.

I know that I'm continuing to develop; philosophically, spiritually, personally,

I am not in the same place I was a decade ago, a year ago, or even six months ago. And as long as that's the case, I will have the confidence to stand up and talk about evolution.

The problem for most people, as I see it, is that they are not moving. They're stuck at some place they reached decades ago.

In an evolutionary worldview, the raison d'être is movement, change.

The highest goodness is actual development.

Are we evolving?

Are we developing?

If we're stagnating, the universe cannot evolve through us.

If we are not moving, the evolutionary process is stagnating.

Of course, it's not something we are deliberately or consciously doing, but because of our ignorance or unenlightenment, we are actually inhibiting the evolution of the interior of the cosmos.

If we have the courage to embrace this radical perspective on ourselves, we awaken to an enormous evolutionary imperative to get moving, *so that the universe can get moving through us.*

From the perspective of a process that is trying to get somewhere, there is always a tremendous urgency—a creative urgency, an ecstatic urgency—for you *to evolve.*

You and I are vehicles through which the process can develop.

Is your self receptive?

Is it open, transparent, surrendered, and committed enough to be a vessel for that creative urgency?

When you get moving, your human body, personality, soul, and spirit becomes an expression and a manifestation of the evolutionary impulse—incarnate and always moving.

The Imperative Quest To Freedom

Andrew Cohen

If you begin to evolve spiritually, at a certain point you awaken to a moral imperative.

You discover an inner compulsion to live for a higher purpose and to actually to do it in public.

This is quite a radical stance to take in the midst of post-modern culture.

Much of postmodern popular spirituality is seen as a very personal, private matter.

Rebelling against the outdated mores of traditional religion, many of us have declared we no longer want to be part of some organized, moral teaching from on high that tells us how to live.

In the age of the individual, spirituality is a private, secret path and it's not something we talk about in public because it's not something that a culture that champions materialism and narcissism gives much validity to.

Evolutionary spirituality, however, is another step forward.

In an evolutionary context we live our spiritual lives in public, because we have realized that our development is not a personal matter.

If we are interested in the future, it's not about me; it's about we.

Evolutionary spirituality is about where we are going.

So now, instead of the personal, private, interior path of the lone individual, spiritual development becomes something we practice in public, because it's about creating the future for all of us.

Perfection

As long as I adhere to a sense of perfection, which would include my body, the body cannot be imperfect; to see only unlimited perfection where limited imperfection seems to be means that *everything* is perfect. [85]

All unhappiness is caused by "our trying to be limited, an ego. The more we are our Self, the happier we are. We will never be completely happy until we are completely being our unlimited and perfect authentic Self." [86]

To quote Sarah Ban Breathnach ...... *The authentic self is the soul made visible.*

---

[85] www.stillnessspeaks.com/sitehtml/llevenson/keystoultimate.pdf (Session 23)

[86] www.stillnessspeaks.com/sitehtml/llevenson/keystoultimate.pdf (Session 24)

Living from the Heart

In the words of Carl Gustav Jung ...... *Your vision will become clear when you look into your heart.* [He] *who looks outside, dreams;* [He] *who looks inside, awakens.*

Spiritual teachers, philosophers and religions have long asserted that one of the most important aspects of being human is to *live from the heart.*

Living from the heart is the true way to live, the life-giving way to live, the spiritual way to live; so, too, does it mean that we have to step outside the dominant governance of the logic and reasoning of the mind, the analytical questioning mind, the self-imposed ego.

While living from the heart may seem like a cliché, the idea of living from the heart is both profound as well as beneficial.

In this secular world of ours, we are taught that intellect is supreme and that we should live from our minds.

It is my belief, my mindset, my paradigm, that authentic living means learning to move our minds away from the ego in order to live from our heart, our center, this deepest place of ourselves that is in tune with our soul.

According to Rollin McCraty, Director of Research at the Institute of HeartMath, the electromagnetic field of the heart is about 5000 times stronger than that of the cranial brain, interacting with and permeating every cell of our bodies. [87]

McCraty's book, <u>The Energetic Heart</u>, explains how the heart carries out the bio-electromagnetic interactions within and between people. [88]

For example, when we are not consciously communicating with others, our physiological systems are interacting in subtle and surprising ways in that the electromagnetic signal produced by our hearts is registered in the brain waves of people around us.

The heart is in fact an important carrier of emotional information and a key mediator of energetic interactions between all living things; when the energy of our hearts is coherent, our bodies change, as do our lives.

---

[87] www.wakingtimes.com/2014/10/13/ancientcoming-heart/
[88] Ibid.

As Osho was so fond of saying ...... *Remember the emphasis on the heart. The mind lives in doubt and the heart lives in trust. When you trust, suddenly you become centered.*

HeartMath INSTITUTE [89]

Effects of Geomagnetic, Solar and Other Factors on Humans [90]

Electrophysiological Evidence of Intuition Part 1: The Surprising Role of the Heart [91] [92]

Electrophysiological Evidence of Intuition Part 2: A System-Wide Process? [93] [94]

---

[89] https://www.heartmath.org/
[90] https://www.heartmath.org/articles-of-the-heart/effects-geomagnetic-solar-factors-humans/#cosmic-rays
[91] https://www.heartmath.org/research/research-library/intuition/electrophysiological-evidence-of-intuition-part-1/
[92] https://www.heartmath.org/assets/uploads/2015/01/intuition-part1.pdf
[93] https://www.heartmath.org/research/research-library/intuition/electrophysiological-evidence-of-intuition-part-2/

Science of the Heart: Exploring the Role of the Heart in Human Performance [95]

Intuitive Wisdom of Our Hearts [96]

Living From The Heart [97]

The Heart is the source of wisdom, truth, peace and love. We call it the Heart because these deeper realities are experienced most strongly in the region of the physical heart; however, the spiritual Heart is not limited to a location in your body. The Heart is the totality of your connection with the essential qualities and greater dimensions of your true nature as a limitless Being. Any full exploration of the larger truth of your Being must include a discovery of the capacities and qualities of this tender, loving and wise aspect of your true nature.

---

[94] https://www.heartmath.org/assets/uploads/2015/01/intuition-part2.pdf
[95] https://www.heartmath.org/research/science-of-the-heart/
[96] https://www.heartmath.org/resources/videos/living-from-the-heart/
[97] endless-satsang.com/images/stories/pdfs/LivingDownload.pdf

Living From The Heart: The Next Step in Evolution [98]

The Heart Has Its Own Brain and Consciousness [99]

GABRIEL GONSALVES

Academy for Applied Heart Intelligence podcasts [100]

Personal Development with the Heart in Mind [101]

---

[98] https://www.learn.hayhouseu.com/wiredtothrive-eg-index1-us
[99] www.wakingtimes.com/2012/09/12/the-heart-has-its-own-brain-and-consciousness/
[100] https://www.appliedheartintelligence.com/podcast/
[101] https://www.appliedheartintelligence.com/

The God Within

It was Yeshua ben Yosef (Jesus) who emphatically stated that the Kingdom of God (or the Kingdom of Heaven) existed within each person.

Buddha described a similar here-and-now state that was available by turning within, but he called it Nirvana.

Both of these reflect the same state of consciousness, one whereby duality has been dissolved and the essential peace and harmony of our being is realized.

Why, then, do we continue to look for a Source that exists outside of ourselves?

In the words of David G. Arenson ...... *The real reality is within. What you see is an illusion, and only reflects what your brain is capable of showing you via its own mechanisms. Technically and physiologically speaking, you're unable to see the truth that you live in an illusion that can equally imprison or free you.*

It is important that each of us maintain this Oneness.

If you are to pray (which admits duality), "it is best to pray for one thing only, *more wisdom*, so that you eliminate all need for any prayer, for any asking." [102]

As it turns out, our very BEingness, our awareness, our consciousness, is the same Source that we seek.

I AM infinite. I AM unlimited.

I AM omnipotent. I AM omniscient. I AM omnipresent.

I do not want, or need, approval from anyone to BE what I AM.

I AM THAT, I AM

---

[102] www.stillnessspeaks.com/sitehtml/llevenson/keystoultimate.pdf (Session 2)

Inspirational Quotes

Albert Einstein

There are only two ways to live your life. One is as though nothing is a miracle. The other is as though everything is a miracle.

Seneca

It is not because things are difficult that we do not dare; it is because we do not dare that things are difficult.

Walt Disney

The sky has never been the limit. We are our own limits. It's then about breaking our personal limits and outgrowing ourselves to live our best lives.

H. Jackson Brown JR

When you can't change the direction of the wind, adjust your sails.

Swami Sivananda

Put your heart, mind, and soul into even your smallest acts. This is the secret of success.

Steve Jobs [103]

Your time is limited, so don't waste it living someone else's life. Don't be trapped by dogma, which is living with the results of other people's thinking. Don't let the noise of other's opinions drown out your own inner voice. And most important, have the courage to follow your heart and intuition. They somehow already know what you truly want to become. Everything else is secondary.

Maya Angelou

My mission in life is not merely to survive, but to thrive; and to do so with some passion, some compassion, some humor, and some style.

Jim Rohn

Happiness is not something you postpone for the future; it is something you design for the present.

———————————✂———————————

William Shakespeare

We know what we are, but know not what we may be.

———————————✂———————————

Ralph Waldo Emerson

What lies behind you and what lies in front of you, pales in comparison to what lies inside of you.

———————————✂———————————

John F. Kennedy

As we express our gratitude, we must never forget that the highest appreciation is not to utter words, but to live by them.

ONLY DO WHAT YOUR HEART TELLS YOU.

- PRINCESS DIANA

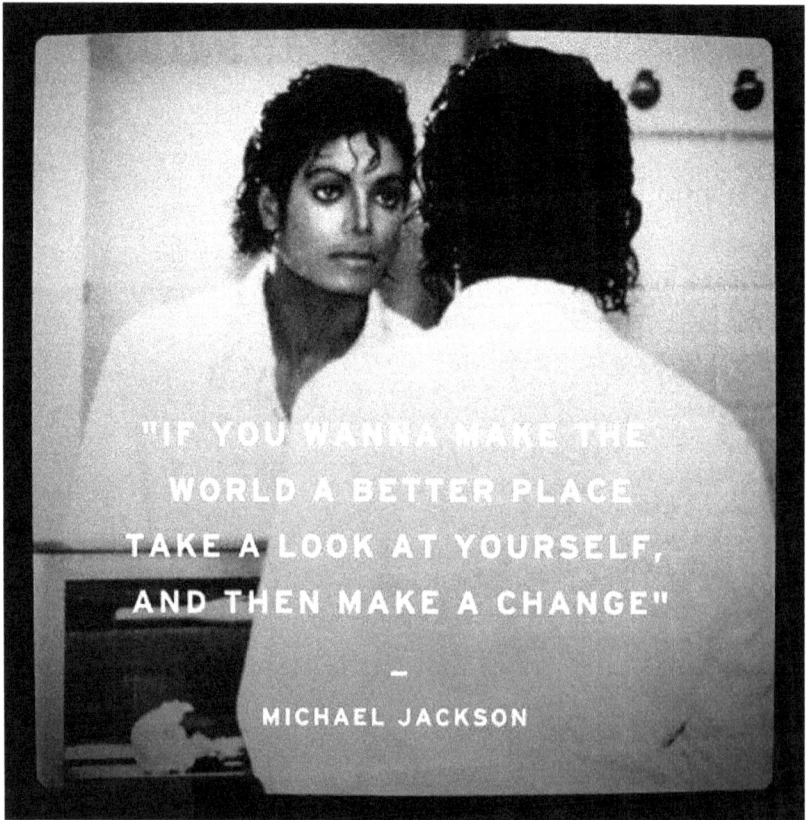

"IF YOU WANNA MAKE THE WORLD A BETTER PLACE TAKE A LOOK AT YOURSELF, AND THEN MAKE A CHANGE"

—

MICHAEL JACKSON

Happiness Quotes

Mahatma Gandhi

Happiness is when what you think, what you say, and what you do are in harmony.

---※---

Ernest Hemingway

Happiness in intelligent people is the rarest thing I know.

Aristotle

Happiness is the meaning and purpose of life, the whole aim and end of human existence.

Alan Epstein

A happy person is not someone to whom "bad" things do not happen. Rather, it is someone who understands that his or her reactions to events are the stuff of happiness.

Marcus Aurelius, Meditations

The happiness of your life depends upon the quality of your thoughts.

Anne Frank, The Diary of a Young Girl

Whoever is happy will make others happy.

Drew Barrymore

I think happiness is what makes your pretty, period. Happy people are beautiful people. They become like a mirror and they reflect that happiness.

Oprah Winfrey

The more you praise and celebrate life, the more there is in life to celebrate.

Daphne du Maurier, Rebecca

Happiness is not a possession to be prized; it is a quality of thought, a state of mind.

Anne Frank, The Diary of a Young Girl

We all live with the objective of being happy; our lives are all different and yet the same.

Aristotle

Happiness is the settling of the soul into its most appropriate spot.

Elizabeth Gilbert, <u>Eat, Pray, Love</u>

People tend to think that happiness is a stroke of luck, something that will descend like fine weather if you're fortunate, but happiness is the result of personal effort. You fight for it, strive for it, insist upon it, and sometimes even travel around the world looking for it. You have to participate relentlessly.

Dalai Lama XIV

Only the development of compassion and understanding for others can bring us the tranquility and happiness we all seek.

Marcus Aurelius, <u>Meditations</u>

Very little is needed to make a happy life; it is all within yourself in your way of thinking.

Susan Polis Schutz

This life is yours. Take the power to choose what you want to do and do it well. Take the power to love what you want in life and love it honestly. Take the power to walk in the forest and be a part of nature. Take the power to control your own life. No one else can do it for you. Take the power to make your life happy.

J. M. Barrie

The secret of happiness is not in doing what one likes, but in liking what one does.

Helen Keller

Happiness does not come from without, it comes from within.

Leo Tolstoy, <u>War and Peace</u>

Pierre was right when he said that one must believe in the possibility of happiness in order to be happy, and I now believe in it. Let the dead bury the dead, but while I'm alive, I must live and be happy.

Lucius Annaeus Seneca

True happiness is to enjoy the present, without anxious dependence upon the future, not to amuse ourselves with either hopes or fears but to rest satisfied with what we have, which is sufficient, for he that is so wants nothing. The greatest blessings of mankind are within us and within our reach. A wise man is content with his lot, whatever it may be, without wishing for what he has not.

Aeschylus

Happiness is a choice that requires effort at times.

Martha Washington

I am still determined to be cheerful and happy, in whatever situation I may be; for I have also learned from experience that the greater part of our happiness or misery depends upon our dispositions, and not upon our circumstances.

Leo Babauta

The way I define happiness is being the creator of your experience, choosing to take pleasure in what you have, right now, regardless of the circumstances, while being the best you that you can be.

Ben Carson

Happiness doesn't result from what we get, but from what we give.

Dale Carnegie

Remember, happiness doesn't depend upon who you are or what you have, it depends solely upon what you think.

Swami Satchidananda, <u>The Yoga Sutras</u>

We are not going to change the whole world, but we can change ourselves and feel free as birds. We can be serene even in the midst of calamities and, by our serenity, make others more tranquil. Serenity is contagious. If we smile at someone, he or she will smile back, and a smile costs nothing. We should plague everyone with joy. If we are to die in a minute, why not die happily, laughing? (136-137).

Fyodor Dostoyevsky

We are all happy if we but knew it.

Boethius

Nothing is miserable unless you think it so; and on the other hand, nothing brings happiness unless you are content with it.

Steve Maraboli, <u>Life, the Truth, and Being Free</u>

Love and compassion are the mother and father of a smile. We need to create more smiles in our world today. Smiles, after all, pave the way to a happy world.

Desiderius Erasmus Roterodamus

The summit of happiness is reached when a person is ready to be what he is.

J. M. Coetzee

The secret of happiness is not doing what we like but in liking what we do.

Tony DeLiso, <u>Legacy: The Power Within</u>

Happiness is part of who we are. Joy is the feeling.

Napoleon Hill

Happiness is found in doing, not merely possessing.

Peter Deunov

Do not look for happiness outside yourself. The awakened seek happiness inside.

Patch Adams

Remember laughing? Laughter enhances the blood flow to the body's extremities and improves cardiovascular function. Laughter releases endorphins and other natural mood elevating and pain-killing chemicals, improves the transfer of oxygen and nutrients to internal organs. Laughter boosts the immune system and helps the body fight off disease, cancer cells as well as viral, bacterial and other infections. Being happy is the best cure of all diseases!

Benjamin Disraeli

Action may not always bring happiness; but there is no happiness without action.

Socrates

He is richest who is content with the least, for content is the wealth of nature.

Jason Mraz

Last weekend a young man asked me how I remain so positive. "It seems all the negativity in the world doesn't affect you," he said. I had no more than a minute with the young man, so I offered this: It's all about where you choose to put your attention, and I choose to be happy.

Democritus

Happiness resides not in possessions and not in gold; the feeling of happiness dwells in the soul.

George Alexiou

You and your purpose in life are the same thing. Your purpose is to be you.

Deepak Chopra

The purpose of life is the expansion of happiness.

Gerald G. Jampolsky, <u>Love Is Letting Go of Fear</u>

You can be right or you can be happy.

Groucho Marx

Each morning when I open my eyes I say to myself: I, not events, have the power to make me happy, or unhappy, today.

Noel Smogard

Happiness isn't a mood; it's a way of life.

Dale Carnegie

Everybody in the world is seeking happiness - and there is one sure way to find it. That is by controlling your thoughts. Happiness doesn't depend on outward conditions. It depends on inner conditions.

Jean-Jacques Rousseau, <u>The Social Contract and Discourses</u>

Why should we build our happiness on the opinions of others, when we can find it in our own hearts?

John Chrysostom

Happiness can only be achieved by looking inward and learning to enjoy whatever life has and this requires transforming greed into gratitude.

Steve Maraboli

When you are living the best version of yourself, you inspire others to live the best versions of themselves.

Oscar Wilde

Pleasure is the only thing one should live for, nothing ages like happiness.

Jean de La Bruyère

The pleasure of criticizing takes away from us the pleasure of being moved by some very fine things.

Ralph Waldo Emerson

To fill the hour – that is happiness.

Mata Amritanandamayi

True happiness is when the love that is within us finds expression in external activities.

John Dewey

To find out what one is fitted to do, and to secure an opportunity to do it, is the key to happiness.

Sophia Adams

Do what makes you happy. Be with who makes you smile. Laugh as much as you breathe. Love as long as you live.

Marcus Aurelius, <u>Meditations</u>

No man is happy who does not think himself so.

Ariel Gore, <u>Bluebird: Women and the New Psychology of Happiness</u>

When we strike a balance between the challenge of an activity and our skill at performing it, when the rhythm of the work itself feels in sync with our pulse, when we know that what we're doing matters, we can get totally absorbed in our task; that is happiness.

Sonia Rumzi

It is not where we are that matters nor what we have, it is what we do with where we are and what we have.

Euripides

The man is happiest who lives from day to day and asks no more, garnering the simple goodness of life.

Tenzin Gyatso

There is no way to happiness; happiness is the way.

Mother Teresa

Be happy in the moment, that's enough. Each moment is all we need, not more.

Steve Maraboli

The disempowered mind believes dreams come true; the empowered mind knows you bring your dreams to life.

Ultimate Freedom Quotes

Vicktor Frankl

Ultimate freedom is a man's right to choose his attitude.

Stephen Covey

There are three constants in life ... change, choice and principles.

Jaggi Vasudev

Meditation is a way of moving into the unlimited dimension of who you are; it is the ultimate freedom.

Dallas Willard

The ultimate freedom we have as human beings is the power to select what we will allow or require our minds to dwell upon.

B. K. S. Iyengar

There is no progress toward ultimate freedom without transformation, and this is the key issue in all lives.

Adyashanti

The ultimate freedom from the nonexistent ego is to see that it is actually irrelevant.

Rajneesh

The desire for total happiness and for ultimate freedom lies dormant in everyone. It is in the form of a seed. It is like a seed that contains a tree within it. In the same way, the fulfillment of man's ultimate desire is hidden in his very nature. In its perfectly developed state, it is our nature to be happy, to be free. Our real nature is the only thing that is true, and only perfecting it can bring complete satisfaction.

Stephen Covey

Our ultimate freedom is the right and power to decide how anybody or anything outside ourselves will affect us.

Freedom Quotes by Osho [104]

---

[104] https://www.osho.com/highlights-of-oshos-world/freedom-quotes-osho

Love Is The New Religion

Knowing that our individual actions collectively decide our fate, the time (and opportunity) is now to accelerate our collective emergence into a new paradigm.

It is time to reclaim what it means to be human.

It is time to immerse ourselves in the sea of possibility and become intentional revolutionaries of compassion, reason, understanding and love.

Quite simply, we are all interconnected; the time to start living life, reflecting this reality, is now.

I have always lived by the Golden Rule; that we are to treat others as we would like to be treated because we are all part of the same whole and any one thing we do to someone else, in truth, we are doing to ourselves.

I do my best to monitor my thoughts, to watch my words, to temper my actions.

The belief that we are separate from one another is presently being challenged both by quantum science as well as our own intuition.

We know in our hearts that the world is supposed to be much more beautiful than what has been offered to us; as the old story of separation falls apart, a new story based on the interconnected web of life is being born. [105]

---

[105] https://wakeup-world.com/2015/07/27/let-the-emergence-of-a-new-humanity-begin/

Through the power of consciousness we are choosing our own reality, and, with that, we have the opportunity to affect a global and transpersonal shift in consciousness that will elevate the human collective to a much higher level of being.

We change the world by changing the story.

I have the power to change my story; so, too, do you have the power to change yours.

Love Is The New Religion (Brian Piergrossi) [106]

---

[106] brianpiergrossi.com/shareit/

Transformation of the Mind

Like Lester Levenson, founder of the Release Technique, [107] I believe that "we are all unlimited beings, limited only by the concepts of limitation that we hold in our minds. These concepts of limitation are not true; furthermore, *because* they are not really true, they can easily be released or discharged." [108]

The Ultimate Freedom: Choosing Your Thoughts [109]

[107] www.lesterlevenson.org
[108] https://www.sedona.com/lesters-story.asp
[109] https://tedmoreno.com/the-ultimate-freedom-choosing-your-thoughts/

The Practice of Humility

From Krishna and Lao Tzu, to Buddha and Jesus, each enlightened master discovered that humility, being open and receptive to all experience, was the key to becoming one with the universe.

Each of us is capable of shifting from the aggressive path of the warrior to the humble path of the sage.

In its quest to protect the self and its desires, the ego forges the illusion of separation; an illusion that creates attitudes of aggression, selfishness and competition (the aggressive path of the warrior).

The key to conscious evolution is humility, the ancient science of mental alchemy that represents The Great Work, the magnum opus, the masterpiece of life; we are here to resurrect the spiritual essence of man that has become trapped in matter.

Every human being participates in alchemy, whether in a conscious manner (through the intentional perfection and manifesting of one's higher nature) or through the tumult and suffering of worldly experiences that finally lead to increased spiritual awareness. [110]

In order to truly partake in The Great Work, the goal for each one of us is to perfect ourselves the best we can through right thinking, right actions and right living; to take the higher path of the soul while we continue to live and operate in the material world. [111]

***

Alchemy Lab [112]

---

[110] https://www.alchemylab.com/great_work_begins_here.htm

[111] https://gnosticwarrior.com/great-work.html

[112] https://www.alchemylab.com/

Spiritual Activism

Spiritual Activism is the coming together of spirituality and activism.

It is not about religion. It is not about any form of dogma.

Spiritual Activism is activism that comes from the heart, not just the head.

Spiritual Activism is compassionate, positive, kind, fierce and transformative.

Being a spiritual activist means taking your part in creating change with a spirit of positivity, compassion, love and a balance of interdependence and self-determination.

Nothing is more inspiring, more rewarding, than being the change we want to see in the world, both within and without.

7 Signs You Might Be A Spiritual Activist [113]

10 Ways To Become A Sacred Activist [114]

---

[113] www.wakingtimes.com/2015/09/30/7-signs-you-might-be-a-spiritual-activist/
[114] www.beliefnet.com/wellness/2009/11/sacred-activist.aspx

The Imperative Quest To Freedom

Can Spiritual Activism Save Humanity? [115]

<u>The Love That Does Justice: Spiritual Activism in Dialogue with Social Science</u> [116]

Sacred Activism (Andrew Harvey) [117] [118]

Spiritual Activism [119]

Spiritual Activism: The Network of Spiritual Progressives [120]

Twelve Keys of Spiritual Activism [121]

Warriors for the Human Spirit [122]

---

[115] https://www.huffingtonpost.com/psyched-in-san-francisco/can-spiritual-activism-sa_b_11420554.html

[116] http://unlimitedloveinstitute.org/downloads/The%20Love%20That%20Does%20Justice.pdf

[117] https://www.andrewharvey.net/sacred-activism/

[118] https://www.youtube.com/watch?v=OyeSac8V3Go

[119] https://www.feminist.com/activism/spiritualactivism.html

[120] https://spiritualprogressives.org/philosophy/spiritual-activism/

[121] humanityhealing.net/guiding-principles/the-12-keys-of-spiritual-activism/

[122] https://margaretwheatley.com/warriors-for-the-human-spirit-training-to-be-the-presence-of-insight-and-compassion/

Authentic Freedom

Freedom, quite simply, is a state of mind.

As long as you give your power away to others, based on your inner beliefs, you are not free to think and choose for yourself.

Being committed to taking back your power, to thinking and choosing for yourself, is what leads to authentic freedom.

Being committed to taking ownership and responsibility for your life is what leads to authentic freedom, and yet, with authentic freedom comes great responsibility.

Sometimes we think we are spiritual and enlightened, but our actions prove the opposite.

We may talk about being authentic and being true to ourselves, but we do nothing to change the status quo.

Authentic freedom equates to living your truth and walking your talk; this gives voice to the authentic self. There no such thing as 50% commitment, or 60%, or 70%, or even 99% commitment; there is only 100% commitment.

Sometimes you have to assert your values, your truth, even if you have to face the consequences of your decision, no matter the cost. You have to stay true to yourself, no matter what. This is the ultimate freedom; the only one we really have.

One of my favorite songs is Walk Your Talk by Robbie Nevil (debut album July 1, 1986). [123]

Authentic Freedom [124]

Two Simple Steps Towards Authentic Freedom [125]

---

[123] https://itunes.apple.com/us/album/robbie-nevil/id1094499140
[124] https://youcanbenew.wordpress.com/2008/04/25/authentic-freedom/
[125] https://fractalenlightenment.com/29116/life/two-simple-steps-toward-authentic-freedom

A New Humanity

Welcome to the inner revolution; a silent revolution.

With the power of your mind and your heart, you are able to create a new world.

❖

6 Shifts In Consciousness We Are All Experiencing Right Now [126]

Activate Your 8th Chakra To Expand Your Spiritual Awareness [127]

Change The Story, Change The World [128]

Creating a New Humanity [129]

---

[126] https://wakeup-world.com/2014/06/13/6-shifts-in-consciousness-we-are-all-experiencing-right-now/
[127] https://www.mindvalleyacademy.com/blog/spirit/eighth-chakra
[128] newstoryhub.com/film/
[129] www.freemeditations.co.uk/newhumanity

New Human, New Earth, New Humanity [130]

The Birth of a New Humanity (Drunvalo Melchizedek) [131]

Visionary and healer Drunvalo Melchizedek discloses never-before-shared information about centuries-old pyramids and temples worldwide.

Witness the birth of a living Unity Consciousness Grid in 2008 that sparked a global transition affecting every human on the planet.

Learn about mankind's evolution out of Atlantis, global development during the last 13,000-year cycle, and what's in store for the new age.

The birth of this new living consciousness grid is for certain the most important story since Atlantis, and yet hardly anyone on Earth is aware that it has happened or what it means for humanity.

---

[130] https://vimeo.com/ondemand/newhuman/157991615
[131] https://www.youtube.com/watch?v=-rkqA1eaFB8

One thing is clear; the outcome of this global consciousness transition is going to affect every single last person on this planet.

If you know what has now become history, your heart can rest knowing that what is to follow in our lives is one of the greatest gifts that Source has given to mankind.

The New Humanity [132]

The New Perception of Community [133]

---

[132] discoursesbymeherbaba.org/v1-17.php
[133] seatofthesoul.com/interviews/oprah-and-gary/

The Ripple (Domino) Effect

A ripple effect is a situation in which an effect from an initial state can be followed outwards incrementally, like ripples that expand across the water when an object is dropped into it.

You may think that you have no effect on the world, but you are the beginning ripple that expands as it extends outward, creating a domino-like affect wherein one tile is built upon the other and they all fall, simultaneously, one after the other.

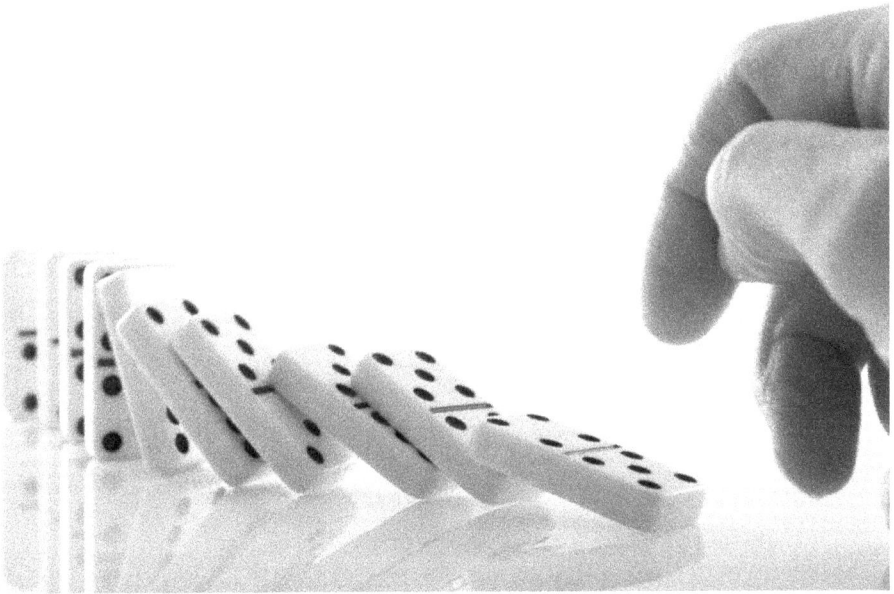

A cumulative effect produced when one event sets off a chain of similar events; it only has to start with you.

The ripple (or domino) effect is not merely a phenomenon that happens to you; it is something you create that heavily influences a chain reaction, sometimes referred to as the snowball effect.

As we continue to start from an initial state of seemingly small significance, putting it out there, the action builds upon itself, becoming larger and more beneficial to all who choose to reap the benefits and continue to pay it forward.

Pay it forward

A Spiritual Revolution

In living the ripple (domino) effect and continually paying it forward, you become your own spiritual revolution, your own spiritual evolution, leading by way of example and demonstrating what is possible.

I believe, profoundly, in the power of humanity.

I believe that we are connected.

I believe that we are a manifestation of a higher power, a higher frequency; this is my visible realization.

I believe that the ultimate truth lies in oneness, love and unity; unfortunately, we are living within a temporary illusion wherein we believe in separate identities.

As long as we continue to hold fast to the cultural narratives that exist, that eschew (renounce) these supposed outlandish ideas, we continue to exhibit naught but greed, selfishness, competition and opposition.

The time to wake-up is now.

The time to change the story, to rewrite the collective narrative, is now.

The time to become what we want to see in the world is now.

http://iamriot.deviantart.com/art/Revolution-of-Love-201739771

My Own State of Being

Mental programming takes years to become entrenched; likewise, it can take just as many years, if not more, to be released.

Anything that serves to shape the mind, to condition the mind, can be considered mental programming: being taught to think a certain way, being taught to act a certain way, being taught to believe (and embrace) a certain philosophy (be it related to education, science, religion, politics, psychology, culture).

Ihzrat Khan, the Sufi Master, once wrote ...... *Life is a continuous succession of problems*.

Of course, so, too, does this mean that the more you think about your problems, the more negative you will become.

I am able to experience freedom when I totally disengage from negative drama and emotion, be it my own and be it one that is being experienced by another. I know that by having been able to disengage, I cannot be drawn into the projected reality.

How do you achieve this disengagement?

[1] Side step the situation.

[2] Focus only on your breathing, for one minute.

[3] Retreat to your peaceful center.

[4] Learn to respond (instead of react).

We are trained to think and behave in a certain way. Whilst I may be triggered by something or someone, the moment that the triggering is over, only I am able to bring about my own upset (anger) or my own happiness.

When someone attacks me, they are merely projecting their own issues, their own unhappiness, their own discomfort, directly onto me.

When I feel uncomfortable inside, I need to learn to acknowledge that feeling, to accept that feeling for what it is, perhaps try and figure out why I am feeling this way, and then let it go.

I may not be able to control what is happening around me, but I can take complete control over what is happening inside of me (what I am feeling, what I am thinking).

The power of choice, the power of reaction, the power of response, is mine alone.

There exists an infinite amount of wisdom that one can tap into; the way to tap into this wisdom often involves some type of meditative practice or introspective journey.

Your wisdom, your true power, is accessible from within; therein lies your personal, independent journey.

I love to pose the question: *How may I be of service?*

When I ask this question, I always get an answer, be it in the form of an impression, a perception, an intuitive knowing.

This is when I find myself taking action, doing my utmost to shine my light as I strive to make a positive difference in the world; shining vibrantly, loving and supporting others.

I know that my higher vibrational frequency, my higher vibrational presence, despite what may be happening in the external, amps up the outward ripple effect. This makes me a wayshower, someone who strives to *walk their talk*, as I continue to work to embody all that is possible.

I am here to live my highest authenticity.

I am here to live an awakened life, an inspired life, a zestful life; one that keeps the highest interest of all beings in mind.

The Power of Presence

Living in the moment, in the now, allows you to bring more presence (whereby you are present) into your own life.

In Eckhart Tolle's words ...... *The most important life lesson to be learned is the realization of who you are in essence, beyond the person.*

When we are continually lost in our thoughts, believing ourselves to be that voice in our heads, we miss the immediacy, the fullness of life, in the here and now.

When you no longer look to the mind to provide you with your sense of identity, you have successfully arrived at the shift that changes everything.

When you have reached that space of consciousness where you become *the observer of your own mind*, you will have realized that you are the awareness behind the thought processes, because your sense of identity now comes from a deeper place.

The moment you become the observer of your own mind is the moment when you understand that the voice in the head (the one that had previously been creating anguish and unhappiness) no longer has power over you.

As the conditioning, the programming, the brainwashing, of the mind begins to subside, you will find that you are able to be with people, with events, with situations, in a non-dysfunctional way, because you are now aligned with whatever arises in the present moment.

Humanity is in the midst of a collective awakening, one that many refer to as the flowering of consciousness. It is up to each one of us to start with ourselves, embracing this shift and allowing the unfolding of something beyond the mind.

As Eckhart Tolle shares ...... *When consciousness flowers, then the human mind is no longer something that creates unnecessary suffering; it becomes something helpful, useful, and potentially capable of achieving miraculous things.*

We become what we practice.

In each and every moment we have a choice to be present or not.

Knowing that we are all connected, this practice of presence may be the kindest action we can take for our own growth and that of humanity; as we change individually, so, too, do we assist in making shifts in the collective experience.

Spiritual Alchemy

Alchemy is the art of transmuting energies, transforming one to the other, and in the process transforming the existing form (lead) into something new (gold).

In reference to physical beings, lead is the base material, meaning "negative thoughts, lustful passions and harmful emotions, which the aspirant of alchemy must change, or transmute, into the spiritual or gold; lead represents the chaotic, heavy and sick condition of metal or the inward man [whereas] gold expresses the perfection of both metallic and human existence," [134] of which pure love is key.

Alchemists believe that everything, including man, can be raised to a higher level of being; this is what is meant by the term *illumination*; a term that also references the death of the earthly (or egoic) self.

---

[134] *Alchemy from the Spiritual Venturer* website accessed on April 2, 2012 at
http://www.denverspiritualcommunity.org/Wisdom/Alchemy.htm

Since the time of Alexandria, ancient sages have long sought ways of transmuting the physical self into the purest form possible.

Spiritual alchemy allows one to break free from the confines of socioeconomic and cultural molds wherein the goal of such a transformation lies in realizing that we are BEings with limitless potential.

Spiritual alchemy is the road-map to self realization; a journey where we must get out of our own way so that we can find (and achieve) the highest possible purity of ourselves.

Spiritual alchemy is concerned with freeing your spiritual self which is trapped within the unrefined parts of yourself (self-destructive personality structures: fears, wounds, belief systems).

Spiritual alchemy, then, is the secret to inner liberation.

You must first identify any self-sabotaging personality behavior that exists (be it self-doubt, stubbornness, pride or arrogance) before advancing to the dissolution stage wherein you one take full responsibility of your perceptions (about yourself, about each other, about the world).

The moment you take ownership, you move from a victim consciousness stage to the realization of your own dictates, your own words; so, too, so you learn to become more aware of your authentic feelings, so that you can honestly see all of your thoughts and feelings for what they are.

This does not mean that we cannot enjoy physical possessions; the problem lies in the significance that they are given.

In order to progress on the spiritual path, one must die to the old way of life (the ego, the illusions, the extravagances); this also includes any aspect of ourselves, and our lives, that no longer serves, or contributes in some way, to this inner work. In doing so, you begin to taste moments of inner peace and stillness that resonate with your soul.

Finding ways to further cultivate living from this place of inner peace and tranquility, even in the most mundane of circumstances, comes next; this is when we experience inner transformation on a profound level (enlightenment).

In keeping with an alchemist saying ...... *Aurum Nostrum Non Est Aurum Vulgi*, meaning our gold is not common gold.

We are here to become whole human beings.

We are here to live the path of the heart.

Dynamic Meditation: How To Access Inner Peace Through Extreme Catharsis [135]

The Seven Stages of Spiritual Alchemy [136]

---

[135] https://lonerwolf.com/dynamic-meditation/
[136] https://lonerwolf.com/spiritual-alchemy/

Do You Believe in Magic?

The only place to be is in the present; the past is but a memory, the future is a dream.

Love is the one feeling that changes everything; everything you knew or thought you knew.

In the words of Khalil Gibran ...... *Love has no other desire than to fulfill itself, but if you love and must needs have desires, let these be your desires; to melt and be like a running brook that sings its melody to the night. To know the pain of too much tenderness. And to bleed willingly and joyfully. To wake at dawn with a winged heart and give thanks for another day of loving; To rest at noon hour and meditate love's ecstasy; to return home at eventide with gratitude; And then to sleep with a prayer for the beloved in your heart and a song of praise upon your lips.*

Nothing is more reverent, more accepting, more humble, than love.

When you begin to change the way you look at things, everything changes.

When you express gratitude, you start to become a giver of joy, of strength, of love.

Live your life in such a way that you know you have made a difference in your own small way.

This is the magic of the universe, an everyday type of magic that connects us all; one that is validated and authenticated by way of uncannily appropriate moments of synchronicity.

The more you believe in this universal magic, the more you see it in transpiring your life, even in the simple things.

With eyes that have been opened, you start to see how everything is connected, you start to see how life is bringing you to the perfect place. Believing in the magic of the universe allows one to stay focused, to trust, to believe.

As written by Roald Dahl ...... *Those who don't believe in magic will never find it.*

Your Mission

Awareness is a state of mind.

Freedom is a state of mind.

Empowerment is a state of mind.

In this during this time that you are here to acknowledge and understand how the mind has been conditioned, corrupted and controlled, by those who deem themselves in power.

Knowledge is power.

Truth is power.

How you use this power determines the course of your life on both a personal level as well as a global (collective) level.

Take the time to investigate.

Take the time to educate yourself.

Continue to use discernment with respect to your findings.

In this also during this time that you are here to learn how to apply this knowledge so that you may begin to re-assert your power, thereby taking charge of your life.

Consciousness is existence.

Consciousness creates.

Consciousness is responsive, alive, intelligent, vibrant, flexible, powerful, caring.

You are consciousness; so, too, are you responsive, alive, intelligent, vibrant, flexible, powerful, caring.

Understanding the power of your belief system (which is mirrored, daily, courtesy of your thoughts, your feelings, your emotions, your actions, your inactions) in conjunction with the power of your mind is critical to grasping the magnitude of your personal power.

It is your mission to become aware of what you think, what you feel, how you react (or respond) and what you say (along with how you voice the message); taking the time to restructure your life with this awareness is key to living a more empowered life, a life of purpose, a life of happiness amidst the chaos.

The choices you make, each and every day, are crucial to your well-being, for that which you think about and focus upon become the primary source for the creation of your reality experience.

Be very clear about your intentions.

When you change your attitude, your perception, and your response(s), you will have changed your life.

THIS IS YOUR LIFE.

DO WHAT YOU LOVE, AND DO IT OFTEN.

IF YOU DON'T LIKE SOMETHING, CHANGE IT.

IF YOU DON'T LIKE YOUR JOB, QUIT.

IF YOU DON'T HAVE ENOUGH TIME, STOP WATCHING TV.

IF YOU ARE LOOKING FOR THE LOVE OF YOUR LIFE, STOP;

THEY WILL BE WAITING FOR YOU WHEN YOU

START DOING THINGS YOU LOVE.

STOP OVER ANALYZING, ALL EMOTIONS ARE BEAUTIFUL. WHEN YOU EAT, APPRECIATE

LIFE IS SIMPLE. EVERY LAST BITE.

OPEN YOUR MIND, ARMS, AND HEART TO NEW THINGS AND PEOPLE, WE ARE UNITED IN OUR DIFFERENCES. ASK THE NEXT PERSON YOU SEE WHAT THEIR PASSION IS, AND SHARE YOUR INSPIRING DREAM WITH THEM.

TRAVEL OFTEN; GETTING LOST WILL HELP YOU FIND YOURSELF.

SOME OPPORTUNITIES ONLY COME ONCE, SEIZE THEM.

LIFE IS ABOUT THE PEOPLE YOU MEET, AND THE THINGS YOU CREATE WITH THEM SO GO OUT AND START CREATING.

LIFE IS SHORT. LIVE YOUR DREAM, AND WEAR YOUR PASSION.

"THE HOLSTEE MANIFESTO" ©2009

The Choice Is Yours

In the astute words of Andrew Cohen ......

If you aspire to become an evolutionarily enlightened human being, your ability to do so depends upon accepting the simple fact that independent of external circumstances, you always have a measure of freedom to choose.

That sounds like a simple statement, but it's amazing how many intelligent people will deny it.

When you look honestly for yourself, however, you will see that it is true: you are always *choosing.*

Sometimes your choices are conscious; sometimes they are unconscious. Sometimes they are inspired by the best parts of yourself; other times they are motivated by lower impulses and instincts.

But the bottom line is that every time you act or react, at some level a choice is being made. And you, whoever you are, are the one who is making that choice.

After all, who else could it be?

Favorite Healthful Recipes

Basking in the rays of superb health also constitutes freedom.

CHAGA

Chaga Peppermint Tea

Having purchased ¼ cup Chaga tea bags from Dwight Thornton in New Brunswick, courtesy of Fiddlehead Heaven Forest Products, [137] [138] I avail of my slow cooker, as per the recipe instructions, [139] filling the cooker with 24 cups of water and simmering, on low, for at least 8 hours; while this means that I use each ¼ cup tea bag just once, I prefer not to have to strain the tea.

---

[137] https://www.fiddleheadheaven.com/
[138] https://www.facebook.com/pages/Fiddlehead-Heaven-Forest-Products/258606057564117
[139] https://www.fiddleheadheaven.com/making-chaga-tea.php

Once cooled, everything is bottled in glass containers and refrigerated. Drinking 4 cups of Chaga daily, this makes for an eight day supply.

One can drink either hot or cold; if hot, one might like to sweeten with honey, lemon, cinnamon, or add a sprig of mint.

When I want some of this specialty drink, I heat up 2 cups of Chaga in a small saucepan and then pour into a cup with a tea dispenser that contains some organic Peppermint Amour from David's Tea. [140] [141]

While Chaga is not an herb, it *is* something that was known to the ancient Chinese emperors.

Chaga is the Russian name for a fungus that you brew to make a drink resembling black tea or coffee (without the caffeine).

---

[140] https://www.davidstea.com/ca_en/home/
[141] https://www.davidstea.com/ca_en/tea/organic-peppermint-amour/10108DT01VAR003979.html

Growing on birch trees, Chaga apparently absorbs the concentrates the immune compounds the birch tree sends to fight its infection.

Extremely rich in antioxidants, it has been scientifically proven that Chaga has anti-cancer benefits; so, too, does it protect against radiation, lower blood pressure, boost the immune system, nourish the liver and help with hypoglycemia.

According to Greg Marley, "one study of Chaga's anti-tumor activity showed that the active anti-cancer components are increased by boiling a decoction and virtually absent in the non-boiled tea. Since a hot water extraction is necessary to access the polysaccharides that stimulate host immune response, I would not recommend the warm water steeping method" (Mushrooms for Health, page 101; by warm he means anything under 212° F). [142]

---

[142] https://www.notastelikehome.org/Chaga.php

According to Cass Ingram, [143] the problem with boiling is that the medicinal components of Chaga (polysaccharides, proteins, sterols, SOD and enzymes including catalase, peroxidase, RNAase and DNAase) are damaged or destroyed by temperatures above 180° F. [144]

As a result, it is important *not* to boil Chaga; this is why I simmer, on low, in a crock pot. With the lid off, the temperature remains steady at 160° F.

Chaga Facts and Benefits [145] [146] [147] [148]

TURMERIC

Turmeric comes from the root of the Curcuma longa plant and has a tough brown skin and a deep orange flesh.

---

[143] www.faim.org/sites/default/files/documents/PPNF-Journal-Chaga.pdf

[144] https://www.notastelikehome.org/Chaga.php

[145] https://www.medicalnewstoday.com/articles/318527.php

[146] https://www.youtube.com/watch?v=aCglNsRCn80

[147] www.raysahelian.com/chaga.html

[148] https://www.youtube.com/watch?v=1gZ-iLRIH9k

Long used as a powerful anti-inflammatory in both the Chinese and Indian systems of medicine, Turmeric was traditionally called Indian saffron because of its deep yellow-orange color and has been used throughout history as a condiment, healing remedy and textile dye. [149]

All You Need To Know About Turmeric [150]

Turmeric Health Benefits [151] [152]

Turmeric Natural News [153]

Anti-Inflammatory Recipe: Salmon with Turmeric [154]

Cancer Kicking Quinoa Dish with Turmeric [155]

---

[149] www.whfoods.com/genpage.php?tname=foodspice&dbid=78
[150] https://www.curejoy.com/content/need-know-aabout-turmeric/
[151] https://www.huffingtonpost.com/andrew-weil-md/turmeric-health-have-a-happy-new-year_b_798328.html
[152] https://www.youtube.com/watch?v=QGgF1cnKdcs
[153] https://www.naturalnews.com/turmeric.html
[154] https://www.youtube.com/watch?v=0gYeZ2yVslo
[155] https://www.youtube.com/watch?v=iK8nOjdW7EA

Chicken Tikka Masala [156]

Chickpea Curry [157]

Curried Winter Soup [158]

Golden Milk [159]

Golden Spinach and Sweet Potato Healthy Sauté [160]

Golden Squash Soup [161]

Gypsy Soup [162]

Indian Style Lentils [163]

---

[156] www.eatingwell.com/recipes/quick_chicken_tikka_masala.html

[157] https://www.allrecipes.com/recipe/34689/chickpea-curry/

[158] https://www.allrecipes.com/recipe/16747/curried-winter-soup/

[159] https://articles.mercola.com/sites/articles/archive/2015/09/21/golden-milk.aspx

[160] www.whfoods.com/genpage.php?tname=recipe&dbid=186

[161] www.whfoods.com/genpage.php?tname=recipe&dbid=33

[162] www.laurieconstantino.com/recipe-index/gypsy-soup/

[163] www.whfoods.com/genpage.php?tname=recipe&dbid=232

Moroccan Chicken [164]

Salmon and Cauliflower Curry with Turmeric [165]

Salmon with Indian Spices [166]

Spiced Kale Scramble [167]

Sweet Glazed Salmon with Roasted Peppers and Turmeric Rice [168]

Tandoori-spiced Grilled Salmon [169]

Turmeric Cauliflower Recipes [170]

------

[164] https://www.allrecipes.com/recipe/18182/moroccan-chicken/
[165] https://lostartskitchen.wordpress.com/2012/10/25/salmon-and-cauliflower-curry-a-nutritional-powerhouse/
[166] www.pbs.org/food/recipes/salmon-with-indian-spices/
[167] https://healyeatsreal.com/spiced-kale-scramble/
[168] https://www.cuisinart.com/recipes/entrees/53.html
[169] https://www.blue-kitchen.com/2012/06/06/one-versatile-spice-rub-two-recipes-part-1-tandoori-spiced-grilled-salmon/
[170] https://recipes.mercola.com/turmeric-cauliflower-recipe.aspx

Turmeric Chicken and Broccoli Stir Fry [171]

Turmeric Poached Salmon with Dill [172]

Turmeric Salmon Recipes [173]

Turmeric Tea [174] [175] [176] [177] [178] [179] [180] [181]

---

[171] https://www.tablespoon.com/recipes/turmeric-chicken-and-broccoli-stir-fry/c79e601d-4166-4b93-8118-2146b72a33e5

[172] https://www.tasteofhome.com/recipes/poached-salmon-with-dill-turmeric/

[173] https://www.yummly.com/recipes/turmeric-salmon

[174] https://www.drweil.com/blog/health-tips/want-to-make-healthy-turmeric-tea-at-home-try-this-simple-method/

[175] https://www.drweil.com/videos-features/videos/how-to-make-turmeric-tea/

[176] https://www.drweil.com/diet-nutrition/nutrition/turmeric-tea-benefits/

[177] https://www.drweil.com/blog/health-tips/know-what-turmeric-can-do-for-you-find-out/

[178] https://autoimmune-paleo.com/anti-inflammatory-turmeric-tea/

[179] https://www.turmericforhealth.com/turmeric-benefits/brew-a-cup-of-turmeric-tea

[180] https://www.meghantelpner.com/blog/tea-time-with-turmeric/

[181] www.primallyinspired.com/turmeric-tea-liver-detox/

Life is the Ultimate Gift

Life is a creative challenge, an opportunity for growth, for expansion, for advancement.

Life gifts you with the freedom to be anything you want to be.

Life gifts you with the freedom to be everything you have the potential to be.

Life is only meaningful for each individual if they find a reason to make it meaningful.

Regardless of whether someone enjoys life or abhors life, the very fact that one can find something to enjoy about life instantly attaches importance (as well as sacredness) to the life they have been given.

The Imperative Quest To Freedom

Humanity is one large consciousness, splitting itself into individuated fragments in order to experience itself fully, and in all ways possible; as a result, life can be viewed as one large experiment wherein each individuated aspect mulls about in order to collect experiences unique to themselves so that these experiences can be added to the overall collection of total experiences that build the ultimate truth of the super consciousness.

In this respect, your meaning is to experience, to participate, to observe, so that humanity, as a whole, continues to grow.

In the words of Mother Theresa ...... *We ourselves feel that what we are doing is just a drop in the ocean, but the ocean would be less because of that missing drop.*

As shared by Elizabeth A. Johnson ...... *Woven into our lives is the very fire from the stars and genes from the sea creatures, and everyone, utterly everyone, is kin in the radiant tapestry of Being.*

What, then, will you decide to do with the gift you have been given?

The true value of something is a direct result of the energy and intent that is put into it.

What is it that you value?

Epilogue

Within the sphere of your own rights, your freedom is, indeed, absolute.

Every individual has the right to the pursuit of happiness, meaning that ......

[1] you have the right to live for yourself

[2] you have the right to choose what constitutes your own private, personal, individual happiness

[3] you have the right to work towards the achievement of your happiness choice

...... as long as you accord the same right to others.

Quite simply, this also means that you cannot be forced to devote your life to the happiness of another.

So, too, does this mean that the societal collective cannot decide that which is to be your purpose, your passion, your choice of happiness. Life circumstances, however, can largely influence this, but only if you let them.

The key is neutrality.

You are here to live your life.

You cannot change the fact that things are always going to happen: good, bad or indifferent (neutral).

Detaching yourself and allowing yourself to see the neutrality in every situation (as opposed to the world being negative or positive) will allow you to free your mind.

Things are merely what they are; hence, freeing yourself from your own constraints of judgement (based on every single thing that happens in your life) is the beginning of a personal revolution.

When you learn to maintain this stance, your awareness is free to focus on what is really important to you; having done so, you stop yourself from wasting valuable energy worrying about the what-ifs.

The individual who patiently (and persistently) walks the unshakable path of neutrality finds that daily life becomes amazingly easy; one part of him (or her) might actively engage in the hurried societal world whilst another part stands serenely aside, bothered by nothing and enjoying everything.

This my friend, is what constitutes true freedom.

Daily OM

To be able to tap in into the divine, to listen to your gut, your intuition, is the birthright that belongs to all of us; unfortunately, so, too, is something that has been bred out of us.

As intuitive beings, we are all born with the same intuitive abilities; it is just that some people have had more practice. Just as exercising makes the muscles stronger, it is possible to strengthen your intuitive abilities.

DailyOM (one of my favorite websites) features a universal approach to holistic living for the mind, body, and spirit, further supporting people who want to live a conscious lifestyle.[182] Founded in 2004 by Madisyn Taylor [183] and Scott Blum, it was born out of their desire to bring the world together by offering messages of consciousness and awareness to people of all walks of life.

---

[182] https://www.dailyom.com/
[183] https://dailyom.com/misc/mt.html

DailyOM Categories [184]

DailyOM Community Discussion Groups [185]

DailyOM Courses [186]

DailyOM Horoscopes [187]

DailyOM Inspirations [188]

Learning to Live: An Instruction Manual (Madisyn Taylor) [189]

Spiritpreneur School: Spiritual Business for Entrepreneurs (free audio podcasts in iTunes) [190]

---

[184] https://dailyom.com/cgi-bin/courses/categories.cgi

[185] https://dailyom.com/community/

[186] https://dailyom.com/cgi-bin/courses/courses.cgi

[187] https://dailyom.com/cgi-bin/display/horoscopes.cgi

[188] https://dailyom.com/cgi-bin/display/inspirations.cgi

[189] www.oprah.com/spirit/introduction-to-dailyom-learning-to-live-course

[190] https://itunes.apple.com/ph/podcast/spiritpreneur-school-for-conscious/id975390187

Mayan Calendar

What follows here is based on several sources: an online May 4, 2017 interview with Carl Johan Calleman [191] as well as his webpage [192] [193] and blog. [194]

---

[191] themindunleashed.com/2017/05/mayan-calendar-expert-says-may-24th-2017-significant-december-21st-2012.html
[192] calleman.com
[193] calleman.com/archive_old_web.htm
[194] calleman.com/blog/

Carl Johan Calleman, one of the world's foremost experts on the Mayan calendar, has written six books based on the framework of the Mayan calendar, which have been translated to a total of fourteen languages.

So, too, has he worked with Mayan elders to help them bring their message out to the world.

According to Calleman, there are nine waves.

9th wave — *Enlightened Unity Consciousness*

8th wave — *Right Brain Dualist Consciousness*

7th wave — *Endarkened Unity Consciousness*

6th wave — *Left Brain Dualist Consciousness*

5th wave — *Enlightened Unity Consciousness*

9th Wave — "Self-Transforming" approach to Life

8th Wave — Self-Authored approach to Life

7th Wave — Socially based approach to Life

6th Wave — "Imperial" relationships

5th Wave — Primal Unity Consciousness

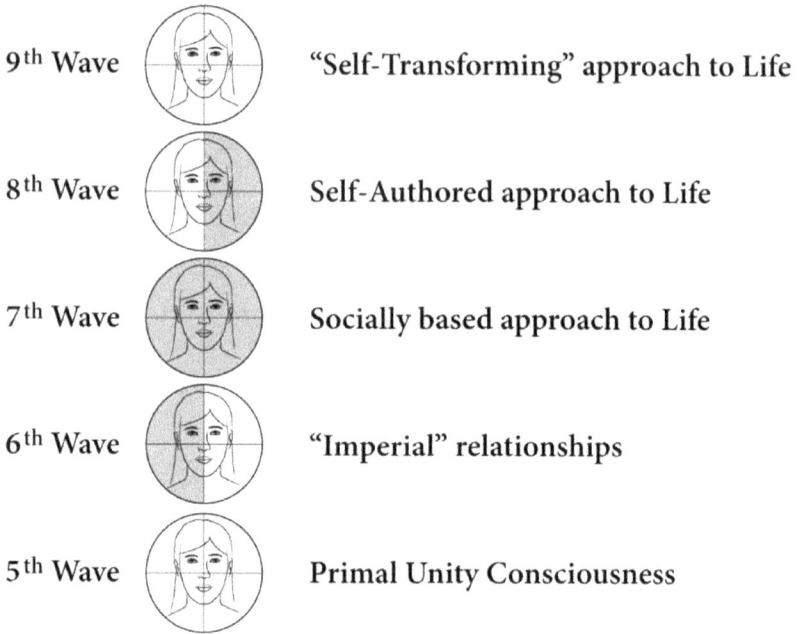

It is important to know what kinds of minds these different waves are creating in the humans that are in resonance with them. From this schemata, it can be understood that the destiny of humanity is to return to unity through a climb to the highest 9th wave. This unity consciousness stands upon a mind carried by the 8th wave, favoring the right (and holistic) brain half, which supports the feminine. The protection and expansion of female rights, worldwide, is thereby a necessary step for manifesting the destiny of humanity.

The Abrahamic religions (Judaism, Christianity, Islam) adhere to the idea that there will be a return to the *Garden of Eden* (meaning a state of unity consciousness).

Whilst such a state will not automatically appear, it *will* result when a sufficiently large number of people have created resonance with the 9th wave. In turn, this requires that an ample number of people already honor the feminine aspect within themselves (8th wave), thereby bringing the yin back into the out-of-balance reality of this physical world.

Even if the 6th wave now appears to be favoring a dark age, in keeping with those who are in resonance with it, there are higher waves that are now active that will counterbalance the effects.

Calleman believes that the most difficult time in this climb to the 9th wave will begin as the 8th wave goes into a night on September 27, 2017.

October 28, 2011 was the day when the nine waves, influencing our biology (and especially our mind) shifted and created a new interference pattern; this means that for the first time, in the history of the universe (including humanity), all waves (the full regalia) were activated and running in parallel.

Before March 9, 2011 the Ninth Wave creating unity consciousness had not been activated and it was only after this shift point that all waves became accessible for us to create resonance with.

Given that each wave creates a different kind of filter for the human mind (see previous images), all will perceive the world differently, depending on which wave they resonate with. In turn, each projects this mind, thereby creating an external reality consistent with the perceptions of their mind.

For example, if we download a mind of duality, we will project this onto the world and create conflicts, but if we download a mind of unity, we will create a world of peace.

What the Mayan calendar ultimately describes are shifting waves with wavelengths of different lengths, sometimes bringing change over very long time periods.

While not a singular event, it can be argued that the chaos in the world has come to a point where it becomes a necessity to create resonance on a larger collective scale with the wave that generates unity consciousness.

Most people today still resonate with the 6th, 7th and 8th wave, none of which creates a fully open heart.

A minority of people have started to develop a resonance with the 9th wave; over time, as they are guided, they will gain a new perception of reality beyond separation.

No event on any single date will bring humanity into the Age of Heart, but the sustained intention to manifest the destiny of humanity through resonance with the 9th wave will serve to create this Golden Age.

People, through their own experiences, will continue to become aware of the existence of the Ninth Wave as they commit to participate in the transformative process, brought by the Ninth Wave, over the years to come.

Carl Johan Calleman [195] is the author of THE PARADIGM SHIFT TRILOGY ......

The Global Mind and the Rise of Civilization (Volume 1) [196]

In each culture the origins of civilization can be tied to the arising of one concept in the human mind: straight lines. Straight and perpendicular lines are not found in nature, so where did they come from?

What shift in consciousness occurred around the globe that triggered the start of rectangular building methods and linear organization as well as written language, pyramid construction, mathematics, and art?

---

[195] https://www.amazon.com/Carl-Johan-Calleman/e/B001K8EGI8/
[196] calleman.com/volume1_old/

Offering a detailed answer to this question, Carl Calleman explores the quantum evolution of the global mind and its holographic resonance with the human mind.

He examines how our brains are not thinking machines, but individual receivers of consciousness from the global mind, which creates holographic downloads to adjust human consciousness to new cosmological circumstances.

He explains how the Mayan Calendar provides a blueprint for these downloads throughout history and how the global mind, rather than the individual, has the power to make civilizations rise and fall.

He shows how, at the beginning of the Mayan 6th Wave (Long Count) in 3115 BCE, the global mind gave human beings the capacity to conceptualize spatial relations in terms of straight and perpendicular lines, initiating the building of pyramids and megaliths around the world and leading to the rise of modern civilization.

He examines the symbolism within the Great Pyramid of Giza and the pyramid at Chichén Itzá and looks at the differences between humans of the 6th Wave in ancient Egypt, Sumer, South America, and Asia and the cave painters of the 5th Wave.

He reveals how the global mind is always connected to the inner core of the Earth and discusses how the two halves of the brain parallel the civilizations of the East and West.

Outlining the historical, psychological, geophysical, and neurological roots of the modern human mind, Calleman shows how studying early civilizations offers a means of understanding the evolution of consciousness.

Spirituality, Altered States of Consciousness and the Shadows of the Mind (Volume 2)

The Future of the Human Mind: Digitalization and Unity with the Divine (Volume 3)

So, too, has he written ......

The 9 Waves of Creation: Quantum Physics, Holographic Evolution and the Destiny of Humanity [197] [198]

In the past few years the world has witnessed changes in social consciousness whose sudden development the ruling scientific paradigm has not been able to explain.

These changes correspond with the activation of new Waves of Creation emanating from the center of the universe that influence human thinking.

From the Big Bang to the present, these Waves guide the evolution of the universe and, through their holographic resonance with the human mind, profoundly shape revolutions in religion, technology, economy, and social consciousness.

---

[197] calleman.com
[198] calleman.com/2017/02/14/the-mayan-nine-waves-of-creation-video/

Presenting a quantum-holographic perspective on world history and human consciousness, Carl Calleman explains the quantum physics behind the Waves of the Mayan Calendar system and how these Waves allow us to understand the shifting eras on Earth as well as the possibilities of the future.

He describes how, prior to the activation of the 6th Wave in 3115 BCE, our social systems were based on a unified cosmic order, but the hologram of this Wave shifted society to an all-consuming focus on Good and Evil, leading to the rise of patriarchal religious structures, slavery, and warfare.

He explores how later Waves and their new holograms helped humanity survive the negative effects of the 6th Wave, such as the Industrial Revolution of the 7th Wave and the Digital Revolution of the 8th Wave.

In 2011, the 9th Wave was activated, bringing with it an accelerated push for a more egalitarian world, a rising awareness of unity consciousness, and access to the full power of all Nine Waves of Creation.

Calleman explains how our individual resonance with each Wave plays a role in the quality of our lives and how we must consciously work to resonate with the higher Waves.

Revealing how we can become quantum activists in a holographic world by aligning with the 9th Wave, the author shows how we each can help manifest the destiny of humanity hinted at in ancient texts.

The Purposeful Universe: How Quantum Theory and Mayan Cosmology Explain the Origin and Evolution of Life

Using recent findings within cosmology, coupled with his broad understanding of the Mayan Calendar, biologist Carl Johan Calleman offers a revolutionary and fully developed alternative to Darwin's theory of biological evolution and the theory of randomness that holds sway over modern science.

He shows how the recently discovered central axis of the universe correlates with the Tree of Life of the ancients.

This provides an entirely new context for physics in general and especially for the origin and evolution of life and suggests that we look upon ourselves as parts of a hierarchy of systems that are all interrelated and evolve in a synchronized way.

Calleman's research demonstrates that life did not just accidentally pop up on our planet, but that Earth was a place specifically tagged for this. He demonstrates how the Mayan Calendar describes different quantum states of the Tree of Life and presents a new explanation for the origin and evolution of consciousness.

Calleman uses his scientific background in biology and cosmology to show that the idea of the Purposeful Universe is real.

He explains not only how DNA but also entire organisms have emerged in the image of the Tree of Life, a theory that has wide-ranging consequences not only for medicine but also for the origin of sacred geometry and the human soul. With this new theory of biological evolution the divide between science and religion disappears.

SPINNING THE LIGHT BLOG (Helen White)

Are You Tuning Into the 9th Wave? [199]

Consciously Creating with the 9th Wave [200]

Using the Nine Waves to Heal Your Life [201]

---

[199] https://spinningthelight.org/2017/04/18/are-you-tuning-in-to-the-ninth-wave/
[200] https://spinningthelight.org/2017/01/29/consciously-creating-with-the-ninth-wave/
[201] https://spinningthelight.org/2017/02/01/using-the-nine-waves-to-heal-your-life/

Flow Consciousness Institute

The Flow Consciousness Institute [202] is a research body dedicated to understanding the mechanics of consciousness, reality and the relationship between the two; using these insights, they are dedicated to developing highly practical tools and trainings for the betterment of humanity and all sentient life. It is their goal to create simple, but powerful, tools and trainings to help individuals create deeply fulfilling, prosperous lives on every level and collectively uplift humanity by shifting planetary consciousness in the direction of greater harmony, peace and self-mastery.

Justin Faerman, co-founder, has written a paper called <u>Mapping the Evolution of Consciousness: A Holistic Framework For Psychospiritual Development</u>. [203]

---

[202] https://www.flowconsciousnessinstitute.com/
[203] https://www.flowconsciousnessinstitute.com/wp-content/uploads/2017/01/Mapping-the-Evolution-of-Consciousness-A-Holistic-Framework-for-Psychospiritual-Development-Ver-2.0.pdf

Recent breakthroughs in the field of quantum physics are revealing that consciousness is primary to our experience of reality, yet there remains no consensus as to the nature of consciousness itself, nor to the nature of reality.

The paper outlines the granular psycho-physiological mechanics of how our individual (and collective) consciousness interacts with, and ultimately shapes, reality in conjunction with other forms of consciousness and quantum information systems from the macrocosm to the microcosm.

Stephen Parato, author of The 8 Stages of Conscious Evolution [204] article, refers to Mapping the Evolution of Consciousness: A Holistic Framework For Psychospiritual Development as map of consciousness; a paper that describes, in plain English, eight stages of consciousness.

---

[204] www.wakingtimes.com/2017/05/31/8-stages-conscious-evolution/

The Joke

KRYON BOOK 10: A NEW DISPENSATION

Page 176

Just like the blood cells carry oxygen, giving life to the Human Being, Humans carry the life of God. And that's the truth! You're actually a piece of the wholeness of what you call God. Spirit cannot exist without you. Every single one of you is an integral piece of divinity, and without you this beautiful tapestry called God wouldn't exist.

~ KRYON

through Lee Carroll, the Original Kryon Channel

Another Simple Reminder

These words, attributed to Lao-Tzu, bear repeating.

If you are depressed, you are living in the past.

If you are anxious, you are living in the future.

If you are at peace, you are living in the present.

Inner peace is one of the key elements in attaining freedom. Whilst Ghandhi's Top 10 Fundamentals for Changing the World [205] is a mentionable read, it is more important to denote that I do my best to live the fundamentals discussed in order to bring peace and change to *my* world because the outer (physical) world always reflects the inner (spiritual).

Take the time to live this moment, right here, right now.

---

[205] https://www.positivityblog.com/gandhis-top-10-fundamentals-for-changing-the-world

Take the time to live this moment with clarity (while still maintaining a sense of humor).

Take the time to live this moment with calmness (while still maintaining a sense of humor).

Take the time to live this moment with positivity (while still maintaining a sense of humor).

Be congruent by living a life of harmony, peace, good will and empathy for such begets tranquility.

Be authentic by living a life true to who you are.

A grateful person is typically a **happier** person.

Gratitude and appreciation begets optimism (which reduces negativity).

Make your acts of gratitude a daily habit.

In the words of John Galt ...... *Do not let your fire go out, spark by irreplaceable spark, in the hopeless swamps of the approximate, the not-quite, the not-yet, the not-at-all. Do not let the hero in your soul perish, in lonely frustration for the life you deserved, but have never been able to reach. Check your road and the nature of your battle. The world you desired can be won, it exists, it is real, it is possible, it's yours.*

We are here to grow, to evolve, to transform, to emerge victorious from this chrysalis, this preparatory or transitional state.

We are here to imagine imagination and consciously create whilst embarking on the journey of journeys.

A personal vision implies taking ownership, taking responsibility, taking action.

A personal vision comes from the self (and does not depend on a group, on a collective, on a hive, on a committee, on a company, on a sector).

A personal vision involves an inner dreaming of deep desire, of passion, of purpose, for this is what constitutes your deliberate entrance point, your conscious entrance point, into the world.

A personal vision is what differentiates you from what the world is proposing. Are you ready to emerge from the group, from the tribe, from the clan, to be who you are meant to be?

Now is the time for a renaissance of your soul.

Thank you for being an errant knight on a mission.

Truth: Chester Bennington

In May 2017, Chester Bennington tweeted: "As of today, my life's purpose is one of love and understanding. The world needs to change and that change comes from within. Hate, pride, vengeance and fear are the plague of the earth. Love, kindness, compassion, empathy and service to others are the cure."

He added a challenge to his followers on Twitter: "Let's all choose to be a part of the cure. If we look outside ourselves to find love and peace we will ultimately fail. It has to come from within. Lead by example."

✦

Having the courage to be yourself, with no past, no future, just living moment to moment, free from imposed ideology; that, my friend, is what constitutes freedom in the truest sense of the word.

Book Bibliography

JAMES ALLEN [206]

WILLIAM WALKER ATKINSON [207]

GENEVIEVE BEHREND [208]

KATE ATKINSON BOEHME [209]

BRENDAN BURCHARD

The Motivation Manifesto

PAULO COELHO

The Alchemist

Warrior of the Light: A Manual

---

[206] newthoughtlibrary.com/allen-james/james-allen-bio.htm

[207] newthoughtlibrary.com/atkinson-william/william-walker-atkinson-bio.htm

[208] newthoughtlibrary.com/behrend-genevieve/genevieve-behrend-bio.htm#TopOfBio

[209] newthoughtlibrary.com/boehme-kate/default.htm#TopOfBio

PANACHE DESAI [210]

A world renowned visionary and transformational teacher, it is through his gift of vibrational transformation [211] that Panache empowers people with the understanding of their limitless nature. As a vibrational catalyst, Panache has dedicated his life to empowering people to free themselves from pain, from suffering, from sadness, from self-limiting beliefs. Through his online programs, live events and book, <u>Discovering Your Soul Signature: A 33-Day Path to Passion, Purpose and Joy</u>, he has touched the hearts of millions and helped them to discover their infinite potential. The insights and vibrational activations that Panache shares are rooted in ancient wisdom combined with modern principles of quantum physics. His perspective is refreshingly non-judgmental, approachable and expansive. Regardless of where life has brought you, he demonstrates that it is possible to open to your limitless nature and the truth of who you are.

---

[210] https://www.panachedesai.com/
[211] Ibid.

Donation Based Programs [212]

Eternal Boundless Love Meditation [213]

Gratitude: Strategies to Bring Your Best Life Into Being (Udemy Course) [214]

Gratitude is one of the most powerful forces for transformation. When you embody gratitude, there is only love. Fear fades away, scarcity no longer exists, separation is bridged and your whole outlook expands.

Ultimately, **gratitude is a choice.**

In essence, it sounds simple, but in practice, it is clear that gratitude is also a learned skill; something you can nourish, cultivate and intimately connect with to harness greater joy, acceptance, present moment awareness, love and freedom.

---

[212] https://www.panachedesai.com/catalog-donation-based
[213] https://www.panachedesai.com/complimentary-access-day-1-divinity
[214] https://www.udemy.com/gratitude-strategies-to-bring-your-best-life-into-being/

Living Breath Awareness Meditation [215]

Your mind is almost always outwardly focused. This is because your senses direct the mind outwardly. The Living Breath Awareness Meditation naturally and easily reverses this process and directs the mind inward — toward the essential Self — the authentic experience of who you are.

Video Teaching: Balance [216]

Balance, in a spiritual sense, is when the authentic Self and the ego are in harmony; we cannot remove the ego completely, but we can be at peace with it.

The ego serves a purpose in our lives, but our conditioning often superimposes an egoic blanket over the totality of our reality. The authentic Self, the Divine within you, seeks the overarching truth of interconnectedness. The ego seeks the illusion of division. Balancing these two counterparts is essential to preparing for transformation.

---

[215] https://www.panachedesai.com/complimentary-access-day-1-living-breath-awareness
[216] https://www.panachedesai.com/metamorphosis-21-day-program-free-gifts

Videos on Facebook [217]

LARRY DOSSEY

<u>Healing Beyond the Body: Medicine and the Infinite Reach of the Mind</u>

<u>One Mind: How Our Individual Mind Is Part of a Greater Consciousness and Why It Matters</u>

HENRY DRUMMOND [218]

RALPH WALDO EMERSON [219]

TIMOTHY FREKE [220]

<u>How Long Is Now? A Journey to Enlightenment and Beyond</u>

---

[217] https://www.facebook.com/pg/panachedesaifanpage/videos/
[218] newthoughtlibrary.com/drummond-henry/henry-drummond-bio.htm#TopOfBio
[219] newthoughtlibrary.com/emerson-ralph-waldo/ralph-waldo-emerson-bio.htm#TopOfBio
[220] timfreke.com

KHALIL GIBRAN [221]

JASON GREGORY [222]

Way of the Weirdo

The Science and Practice of Humility: The Path to Ultimate Freedom

Enlightenment Now: Liberation Is Your True Nature

Fasting the Mind: Spiritual Exercises for Psychic Detox

THICH NHAT HANH [223] [224] [225]

The Miracle of Mindfulness

CHARLES HAANEL [226]

---

[221] newthoughtlibrary.com/gibranKhalil/bio_gibran.htm#TopOfBio
[222] https://jasongregory.org
[223] https://plumvillage.org/about/thich-nhat-hanh/
[224] www.buddhanet.net/masters/thich.htm
[225] www.oprah.com/spirit/oprah-talks-to-thich-nhat-hanh
[226] newthoughtlibrary.com/haanel-charles/bio_haanel.htm

HARRY HAMBLIN [227]

NAPOLEON HILL [228]

ANODEA JUDITH

The Sevenfold Journey: Reclaiming Mind, Body and Spirit Through the Chakras

JON KABAT-ZINN [229] [230]

Guided Mindfulness Meditation (audio CD)

Guided Mindfulness Meditation Series 2 (audio CD)

Guided Mindfulness Meditation Series 3 (audio CD)

Mindfulness for Beginners: Reclaiming the Present Moment and Your Life

Mindfulness Meditation: Cultivating the Wisdom of Your Body and Mind (audio CD)

---

[227] newthoughtlibrary.com/hamblinHarry/bio_hamblin.htm#TopOfBio
[228] newthoughtlibrary.com/hillNapoleon/bio_hill.htm#TopOfBio
[229] https://www.mindfulnesscds.com/
[230] https://www.mindful.org/jon-kabat-zinn-defining-mindfulness/

VISHEN LAKHIANI

Realizing that there was great potential for meditation and personal development in the digital world, Vishen launched Mindvalley in 2003 (with former partner Mike Reining) as a digital publisher and marketer of self-help programs and courses, building the company with zero angel investors, venture capitalist money and government grants.

Through Mindvalley, he builds businesses that innovate on transformational education geared towards positive impact for all ages; the company's mission is to empower people to live healthier and happier lives, unleash their fullest potential and Be Extraordinary by introducing them to tools and ideas that are currently missing from traditional education systems.

Vishen Lakhiani [231] is an entrepreneur, an education technology innovator, a motivational speaker as well as a philanthropist.

---

[231] www.vishenlakhiani.com/about

40 Years of Zen [232]

CHRISTIAN LARSON [233]

BARBARA HOBERMAN LEVINE

<u>Your Body Believes Every Word You Say: The Language of the Body/Mind Connection</u>

JED McKENNA [234]

<u>Spiritual Enlightenment, The Damnedest Thing</u> (Book 1)

<u>Spiritually Incorrect Enlightenment</u> (Book 2)

<u>Spiritual Warfare</u> (Book 3)

<u>Jed McKenna's Theory of Everything: The Enlightened Perspective</u>

<u>Dreamstate: A Conspiracy Theory</u>

---

[232] blog.mindvalleyacademy.com/vishen-lakhiani/40-years-of-zen
[233] newthoughtlibrary.com/larsonChristian/bio_larson.htm#TopOfBio
[234] www.wisefoolpress.com/

DAN MILLMAN [235]

<u>Body Mind Mastery</u>

<u>Way of the Peaceful Warrior</u>

GARY QUINN

<u>Living in the Spiritual Zone: 10 Steps to Change Your Life and Discover Your Truth</u>

<u>The YES Frequency: Master a Positive Belief System and Achieve Mindfulness</u>

FLORENCE SCOVEL SHINN [236]

ELDON TAYLOR

<u>Gotcha: The Subordination of Free Will</u>

---

[235] www.peacefulwarrior.com/
[236] newthoughtlibrary.com/shinn-florence-scovel/florence-scovel-shinn-bio.htm#TopOfBio

BRIAN THOMPSON

A Zen vegan poet, Brian lives on a mountain by the sea, writing about our common state of being, non-duality and infinity. The author of <u>Sparks to Awaken</u>, his work explores the nature of conscious awareness and offers personal insight into the spiritual practices of self-inquiry, self-awareness, mindfulness and achieving inner stillness.

The webmaster of Zen Thinking, [237] it is here you will find profound pointers to help you awaken to your own true Self; one that is free from self-inflicted suffering.

With teachings that are dogma-free, inspired through the ancient non-dual wisdom of Zen, Advaita, Buddhism and Taoism, everything Brian offers is an expression of his own experiential understandings.

---

[237] www.zenthinking.net

ECKHART TOLLE

Born in Germany and educated at the Universities of London and Cambridge, it was at the age of 29 that Eckhart experienced a profound inner transformation that radically changed the course of his life.

The next few years were devoted to understanding, integrating and deepening that transformation, which marked the beginning of an intense inward journey.

His written works include two New York Times bestsellers, both widely regarded as among the most influential spiritual books of our time: the Oprah's Book Club selection, <u>A New Earth</u>, [238] and <u>The Power of Now</u>, which has been translated into more than 30 languages.

---

[238] www.oprah.com/own-a-new-earth/an-excerpt-from-a-new-earth-by-eckhart-tolle

The Power of Presence: An 8 Week Training Course Fpr Awakening Consciousness and Living in the Now [239]

Video 1: Why Presence?

Eckhart tells us that the arising of Presence is *no longer a luxury, but a necessity* and *the most important thing that can happen in your lifetime.*

Video 2: Love and Presence

Eckhart discusses love in the conventional sense and the transformational power of Presence in our relationships.

Video 3: Practicing Presence

Bringing Presence into our daily lives and activities is about having a friendly attitude toward whatever arises in the moment; something that we can all learn and get better at perfecting.

---

[239] https://www.soundstrue.com/store/power-of-presence/eckhart-tolle-webinar

Video 4: Live Webinar

Eckhart answers viewer questions about the practice of Presence.

RALPH WALDO TRINE [240]

THOMAS TROWARD [241]

WALLACE D. WATTLES [242]

KEN WILBER

Widely regarded as the *Einstein of Consciousness* and the *Aristotle of our Time*, Ken Wilber is a living legend. He was a 19-year old Masters student when his journey to greatness began.

Fed up with academia, he became obsessed with understanding the human condition and our highest potentials.

---

[240] newthoughtlibrary.com/trineRalphWaldo/bio_trine.htm#TopOfBio

[241] newthoughtlibrary.com/trowardThomas/bio_troward.htm#TopOfBio

[242] newthoughtlibrary.com/wattlesWallace/wallace-wattles-bio.htm#TopOfBio

He wanted to know what was ultimately true, how everything fit together, the real source of fulfillment for human life. Not getting answers from his college professors, he left grad school and set out on an epic journey to discover them for himself.

When he was 23 years old, he published his first book, <u>The Spectrum of Consciousness</u>, the results of his four years of in-depth study.

This groundbreaking synthesis of religion, philosophy, physics, and psychology started a revolution in transpersonal psychology.

He was the first to suggest in a systematic way that the great psychological systems of the West could be integrated with the noble contemplative traditions of the East.

<u>The Spectrum of Consciousness</u>, first released by Quest in 1977, has been the prominent reference point for all subsequent attempts at integrating psychology and spirituality.

Some of my personal favorite book titles are ......

No Boundary: Eastern and Western Approaches to Personal Growth (February 2001)

Wicked & Wise: How to Solve the World's Toughest Problems (Wicked and Wise) (August 2015)

Integral Meditation: Mindfulness as a Way to Grow Up, Wake Up, and Show Up in Your Life (March 2016)

A Brief History of Everything (20th Anniversary Edition) (May 2017)

The Religion of Tomorrow: A Vision for the Future of the Great Traditions: More Inclusive, More Comprehensive, More Complete (May 2017)

Your Superhuman Potential [243]

---

[243] https://yoursuperhumanpotential.com/ecm-download/

PARAMAHANSA YOGANANDA [244]

GARY ZUKAV and LINDA FRANCIS

From The Oprah Winfrey Show to their New York Times Bestselling books, the humor, intimacy, and wisdom of Gary Zukav and Linda Francis have helped millions of people create authentic power and transform their lives.

Seat of the Soul Institute [245]

You are the key to your own treasure.

---

[244] newthoughtlibrary.com/yogananda/bio_yogananda.htm#TopOfBio

[245] seatofthesoul.com/about/seat-of-the-soul-institute/

Website Bibliography

In words that have been attributed to St. Bernard de Clairvaux ......*There are those who seek knowledge for the sake of knowledge; that is curiosity. There are those who seek knowledge to be known by others; that is vanity. There are those who seek knowledge in order to serve; that is love.*

In the words of Norman Vincent Peale .... *Change your thoughts and you change your world.*

AFFORMATIONS

Afformations [246]

Combining EFT and Afformations [247]

---

[246] www.suzannebrothers.com/site/wp-content/uploads/2010/11/afformations.pdf
[247] www.eftzone.com/2007/05/14/combining-eft-afformations/

Happyecho's Huge List of Positive Afformations [248]

ARTICLES

Happiness: The Mind's Bottom Line [249]

BELIEF SYSTEMS

7 Limiting Beliefs Keeping You From Living Your Best Life [250]

Beliefs Create Your Reality, But What Creates Beliefs [251]

Changing Core Beliefs, Emotional Reactions and Behaviors [252]

Cognitive Therapy 101: Core Beliefs [253]

_____

[248] https://happyecho.com/wp-content/uploads/2015/06/DAna%E2%80%99s-Huge-List-of-Positive-Afformations.pdf

[249] https://www.peterrussell.com/WUIT/Happiness.php

[250] https://personalexcellence.co/blog/limiting-beliefs/

[251] www.the-secret-of-manifestation.org/beliefs-create-reality-creates-beliefs.html/

[252] www.pathwaytohappiness.com/writings_falsebeliefs.htm

[253] rosspsychology.com/blog/cognitive-therapy-101-core-beliefs

Dissolving Limiting Beliefs [254]

Do You Determine Your Beliefs or Do Your Beliefs Determine You (Part 1)? [255]

Do You Determine Your Beliefs or Do Your Beliefs Determine You (Part 2)? [256]

Do You Determine Your Beliefs or Do Your Beliefs Determine You (Part 3)? [257]

Do Your Beliefs Empower You or Limit You? [258]

Examples of Limiting Beliefs [259]

---

[254] https://www.stevepavlina.com/blog/2012/07/dissolving-limiting-beliefs/

[255] https://www.lifehack.org/articles/lifestyle/do-you-determine-your-beliefs-or-do-your-beliefs-determine-you-part-one.html

[256] https://www.lifehack.org/articles/lifestyle/do-you-determine-your-beliefs-or-do-your-beliefs-determine-you-part-two.html

[257] https://www.lifehack.org/articles/lifestyle/do-you-determine-your-beliefs-or-do-your-beliefs-determine-you-part-three.html

[258] https://www.lifehack.org/articles/lifestyle/do-your-beliefs-empower-you-or-limit-you.html

[259] https://www.2knowmyself.com/limiting_beliefs_examples

How To Change Limiting Beliefs [260]

How To Change Your Core Beliefs In 9 Steps [261]

How To Identify Core Beliefs [262]

How To Kill The Root Of A Limiting Belief [263]

How To Rise Above Social Conditioning and Live An Amazing Life [264]

Human Mental Programming Levels [265]

Identifying and Overcoming Limiting Beliefs [266]

---

[260] www.myrkothum.com/how-to-change-self-limiting-beliefs/
[261] https://lonerwolf.com/how-to-change-your-core-beliefs/
[262] www.pathwaytohappiness.com/writings_core_beliefs.htm
[263] https://liveboldandbloom.com/02/health/how-to-kill-the-root-of-a-limiting-belief
[264] iameduard.com/socialconditioning/
[265] https://is.muni.cz/el/1456/podzim2006/KHMA2/um/2822691/Hofstede.pdf
[266] www.goal-setting-motivation.com/set-your-goals/overcoming-limiting-beliefs/

---

[267] https://www.stevepavlina.com/blog/2006/07/installing-empowering-beliefs/
[268] changingminds.org/explanations/belief/limiting_beliefs.htm
[269] https://eddinscounseling.com/wp-content/uploads/25reversingcorebeliefs.pdf
[270] https://www.lifehack.org/articles/featured/subjective-reality.html
[271] https://www.lifehack.org/articles/featured/take-back-your-personal-power-part-1.html
[272] https://www.lifehack.org/articles/featured/take-back-your-personal-power-part-2.html
[273] https://trans4mind.com/spiritual/brainwashing.htm

The Case of the Conditioned Mind: A New Curriculum for Questioning Minds (ages 9 to 14) [274]

The Complete Guide On How To Overcome Your Limiting Beliefs [275]

The Five Limiting Beliefs That Hinder Your Success [276]

Typical Negative Core Beliefs [277]

BODY MIND SPIRIT CONNECTION

Your Body is the Mirror of Your Life [278]

WellBeing Alignment [279]

---

[274] https://www.atriumsoc.org/samples/Curricula_ConditionedMind-Sample.pdf
[275] https://blog.iqmatrix.com/limiting-beliefs
[276] https://www.qimacros.com/knowware-articles/five-limiting-beliefs/
[277] www.core-beliefs-balance.com/example_negative_core_beliefs.htm
[278] educate-yourself.org/mbc/mbcbodymirroroflife8jun02.shtml
[279] https://www.wellbeingalignment.com/

COMPASSIONATE COMMUNICATION

Words Can Change Your Brain [280]

CONSCIOUSNESS

An Exploration of Quantum Consciousness [281]

Consciousness and Quantum Reality [282]

Consciousness and the Quantum [283]

Consciousness as a Fundamental Building Block of the Universe [284]

Consciousness as a Sub-Quantum Phenomena [285] [286]

---

[280] https://brainworldmagazine.com/newberg-waldmans-compassionate-communication/

[281] www.quantumconsciousness.org/content/overview-sh

[282] www.intuition.org/txt/herbert.htm

[283] www.markbancroft.com/info/quantum-consciousness

[284] https://www.scienceandnonduality.com/consciousness-as-fundamental-building-in-the-universe/

[285] https://www.cfpf.org.uk/articles/rdp/caasqp/caasqp.html

[286] www.survivalafterdeath.info/articles/pearson/consciousness.htm

Consciousness Creates Reality: Physicists Admit The Universe Is Immaterial, Mental and Spiritual [287]

Consciousness, Numbers and the Laws, Principles and Particles of Physics: What is the Fundamental Nature of the Universe? [288]

Could Life and Consciousness Be Related To The Fundamental Quantum Nature of the Universe? [289]

Does Consciousness Affect Matter? [290]

Fundamental Physics of Consciousness [291]

---

[287] https://www.collective-evolution.com/2014/11/11/consciousness-creates-reality-physicists-admit-the-universe-is-immaterial-mental-spiritual/

[288] https://medium.com/@MCStannard/consciousness-numbers-and-the-laws-principles-and-particles-of-physics-what-is-the-fundamental-5cee6715b85a

[289] www.quantumconsciousness.org/content/overview-sh

[290] themindbodyspiritblog.com/does-consciousness-affect-matter/

[291] www.geneman.com/pubs/physics_fqxi2/fundamental_physics_of_consciousness.htm

Mind Before Matter: How Consciousness is Making a Comeback Through Scientific Exploration [292]

Noetics: A proposal for a theoretical approach to consciousness [293]

Physicalism: A False View of the World [294]

Quantum Approaches to Consciousness [295]

The Strangle Link Between the Human Mind and Quantum Physics [296]

The Universe May Be Conscious, Says Prominent Scientists [297]

---

[292] https://wakeup-world.com/2015/10/01/mind-before-matter-how-consciousness-is-making-a-comeback-through-scientific-exploration/

[293] georgezarkadakis.com/2011/05/20/noetics-a-proposal-for-a-theoretical-approach-to-consciousness/

[294] www.realitysandwich.com/physicalism_false_view_world

[295] https://plato.stanford.edu/entries/qt-consciousness/

[296] www.bbc.com/earth/story/20170215-the-strange-link-between-the-human-mind-and-quantum-physics

[297] https://bigthink.com/philip-perry/the-universe-may-be-conscious-prominent-scientists-state

DNA

Can You Change Your DNA? [298]

DNA Report (Gregg Braden) [299]

Emotions Can Change Your DNA [300]

Emotions, DNA and the Divine Matrix [301]

Human Emotions Can Change DNA (Gregg Braden) [302]

Part 3: The Link Between Emotions and DNA [303]

You Can Change Your DNA [304]

----

[298] https://www.care2.com/greenliving/can-you-change-your-dna.html
[299] https://www.bibliotecapleyades.net/mistic/esp_greggbraden_11.htm
[300] https://www.care2.com/greenliving/emotions-can-change-your-dna.html
[301] www.atlanteanconspiracy.com/2013/04/emotions-dna-and-divine-matrix.html
[302] https://www.youtube.com/watch?v=pq1q58wTolk
[303] https://www.youtube.com/watch?v=WenDDMWYM3U
[304] https://www.heartmath.org/articles-of-the-heart/personal-development/you-can-change-your-dna/

We Create Our Reality By Choosing It With Our Feelings [305]

DR. MASARU EMOTO

Dr. Emoto Believed that Water *Is Something Not Of This Earth* [306]

EFT TAPPING

EFT Tapping Charts [307]

EFT Tapping Points [308]

EFT: The Basic Recipe [309]

EFT Video Library [310]

---

[305] https://www.linkedin.com/pulse/we-create-our-reality-choosing-feelings-louise-yoga

[306] https://www.wakingtimes.com/2015/09/30/dr-masaru-emoto-believed-that-water-is-something-not-of-this-earth/

[307] www.tapintoheaven.com/charts/

[308] www.theenergytherapycentre.co.uk/tapping-points.htm

[309] www.bradyates.net/eft.html

[310] https://eft.mercola.com

How To Do The EFT Tapping Basics [311]

What Is EFT: Theory, Science and Uses [312]

What Is Tapping And How Can I Start Using It? [313]

FREE COURSES

Hidden Knowledge Course [314]

Insight Course [315]

Inspiration Course [316]

Law of Emergence Audio-course [317]

Transformation Course [318]

---

[311] https://www.emofree.com/eft-tutorial/tapping-basics/how-to-do-eft.html
[312] https://www.emofree.com/eft-tutorial/tapping-basics/what-is-eft.html
[313] https://www.thetappingsolution.com/what-is-eft-tapping/
[314] https://www.hidden-knowledge.net
[315] https://www.insightcourse.net
[316] https://www.inspirationcourse.net
[317] lawofemergence.com/free-audio-course
[318] https://www.transformationteam.net

FREE INSPIRATIONAL MOVIES

3 Magic Words [319]

Carrots, Eggs or Coffee Beans [320]

Change Is Good: You Go First [321]

Dreams are Whispers From the Soul [322]

Finding Joy [323]

Gratitude: The Short Film [324]

Learning to Dance in the Rain [325]

Life is Like Coffee [326]

---

[319] https://3magicwordsmovie.com
[320] www.flickspire.com/m/Rubbertree669/CarrotsEggsCoffee
[321] https://play.simpletruths.com/movie/change-is-good/
[322] https://play.simpletruths.com/movie/dreams-are-whispers-from-the-soul/
[323] www.flickspire.com/m/Rubbertree669/FindingJoy
[324] https://vimeo.com/44131171
[325]
www.flickspire.com/m/Rubbertree669/LearningToDanceInTheRain
[326] www.flickspire.com/m/Rubbertree669/LifeIsLikeCoffee

Make A Difference [327]

May You Be Blessed [328]

No Glass Ceiling, Just Blue Sky [329]

Persevere [330]

Road to Happiness [331]

The Butterfly Effect [332]

The Dash [333]

The Power of Acknowledgment [334]

The Power of Attitude [335]

---

[327] makeadifferencemovie.com/index.php
[328] https://play.simpletruths.com/movie/may-you-be-blessed/
[329] https://play.simpletruths.com/movie/no-glass-ceiling-just-blue-sky/
[330] www.flickspire.com/m/Rubbertree669/Persevere
[331] www.flickspire.com/m/LittleeInc/RoadToHappiness/
[332] www.flickspire.com/m/LittleeInc/ButterflyEffect
[333] www.flickspire.com/m/LittleeInc/TheDash
[334] acknowledgmentmovie.com/index.php
[335] www.flickspire.com/m/Rubbertree669/PowerOfAttitude

The Strangest Secret [336]

Top Motivational Videos [337]

Words of Gratitude [338]

GUIDED MEDITATION

The Guided Meditation Site [339]

INSPIRATIONAL (SPIRITUAL) MOVIES

Bruce Almighty

A guy who complains about God too often is given almighty powers to teach him how difficult it is to run the world.

Forrest Gump

Forrest Gump, while not intelligent, has accidentally been present at many historic moments, but his true love, Jenny Curran, eludes him.

---

[336] www.flickspire.com/m/LittleeInc/TheStrangestSecret
[337] https://www.simpletruths.com/movies.html
[338] www.flickspire.com/m/MBT/WordsOfGratitude
[339] https://www.the-guided-meditation-site.com

Inception

A skilled extractor is offered a chance to regain his old life as payment for a task considered to be impossible.

Kumaré

A documentary about a man who impersonates a wise Indian Guru and builds a following in Arizona. At the height of his popularity, the Guru Kumaré must reveal his true identity to his disciples and unveil his greatest teaching of all.

Life Is Beautiful

In 1930s Italy, a carefree Jewish book keeper named Guido starts a fairy tale life by courting and marrying a lovely woman from a nearby city. Guido and his wife have a son and live happily together until the occupation of Italy by German forces.

In an attempt to hold his family together and help his son survive the horrors of a Jewish Concentration Camp, Guido imagines that the Holocaust is a game and that the grand prize for winning is a tank.

Pay It Forward

A young boy attempts to make the world a better place after his teacher gives him that chance.

Shawshank Redemption

Two imprisoned men bond over a number of years, finding solace and eventual redemption through acts of common decency.

Spring, Summer, Fall, Winter... and Spring

This film takes place in an isolated lake, where an old monk lives on a small floating temple. The wise master has also a young boy with him that teaches to become a monk. And we watch as seasons and years pass by.

The Bucket List

Two terminally ill men escape from a cancer ward and head off on a road trip with a wish list of to-dos before they die.

The Matrix

A computer hacker learns from mysterious rebels about the true nature of his reality and his role in the war against its controllers.

The Peaceful Warrior

A chance encounter with a stranger changes the life of a college gymnast.

Yes Man

A guy challenges himself to say YES to everything for an entire year.

INTUITION

18 Ways To Strengthen Your Intuition [340]

---

[340] https://www.mindbodygreen.com/0-17693/18-ways-to-strengthen-your-intuition.html

---

[341] https://www.consciouslifestylemag.com/intuition-developing-exercises/

[342] https://cauldronsandcupcakes.com/2012/09/16/strengthening-intuition-a-program-of-exercises/

[343] https://www.takingcharge.csh.umn.edu/activities/exercises-developing-your-intuition

[344] www.au.af.mil/au/awc/awcgate/army/rotc_self-aware.pdf

[345] https://www.brainpickings.org/2014/01/27/alan-watts-taboo/

MEANINGFULNESS

A Meaningful Life in a Meaningless Cosmos: Two Rival Approaches [346]

The Real Battle: Meaningful versus Meaningless [347]

METAPHYSICAL PROGRAMS

American Metaphysical Doctors Association [348]

Consciousness and the Conscious Universe [349]

Descriptive Metaphysics [350]

International College of Metaphysical Theology [351]

---

[346] cosmosandhistory.org/index.php/journal/article/view/52/104
[347] spiritualperception.org/the-real-battle-meaningful-vs-meaningless/
[348] https://universityofmetaphysics.com/american-metaphysical-doctors-association/
[349]

https://www.bibliotecapleyades.net/ciencia/ciencia_consciousuniverse.htm
[350] www.sdp.org/sdp/spirit/metaphysics.html
[351] www.metaphysicscollege.com

International Metaphysical University [352]

Maharishi University of Management [353]

Metaphysical Society [354]

Metaphysics by Aristotle [355]

Metaphysics For Life [356]

Metaphysics Institute [357]

School of Metaphysics [358] [359]

Sofia University: The Institute of Transpersonal Psychology [360]

---

[352] https://intermetu.com
[353] https://www.mum.edu/ba-in-consciousness-and-human-potential
[354] www.metaphysicalsociety.com
[355] classics.mit.edu/Aristotle/metaphysics.html
[356] www.metaphysics-for-life.com/
[357] https://www.metaphysicsinstitute.org
[358] https://www.schoolofmetaphysics.com
[359] https://www.schoolofmetaphysics.com/practitioner-training/
[360] https://www.sofia.edu

The Metaphysical Institute of Higher Learning [361]

University of Oxford: Reality, Being and Existence [362]

University of Metaphysical Sciences [363]

University of Metaphysics [364]

University of Sedona [365]

METAPHYSICS

Science of the Sages: Nothing Stands Apart [366]

Science and the Gita [367]

Spiritual Alchemy [368]

---

[361] https://metaphysicalinstitute.net
[362] https://www.conted.ox.ac.uk/courses/reality-being-and-existence-an-introduction-to-metaphysics-online?code=V500-6
[363] https://metaphysicsuniversity.com
[364] https://universityofmetaphysics.com
[365] https://universityofsedona.com
[366] www.advaita.org.uk/extracts/science_wolfe.html
[367] www.hinduwisdom.info/articles_hinduism/287.htm
[368] dreamcatcherreality.com/spiritual-alchemy/

The Physicist as Mystic [369]

What The Bleep Are They On About? [370]

You Are a Hologram: The Holographic Nature of Consciousness and Reality [371]

MINDFULNESS

Eating Meditation: A Mindfulness Worksheet [372]

Mindful Eating [373]

Mindfulness At Work [374]

Mindfulness Exercises [375]

Mindfulness Talks and Meditations [376]

----

[369] https://www.luisprada.com/the_physicist_as_mystic/
[370] www.abc.net.au/science/articles/2005/06/30/2839498.htm
[371] https://thestillmind.wordpress.com/tag/subatomic-particles/
[372] https://mindfulnessexercises.com/eating-meditation/
[373] https://mindfulnessexercises.com/music/mindful-eating/
[374] https://mindfulnessexercises.com/music/real-happiness-work/
[375] https://mindfulnessexercises.com
[376] https://mindfulnessexercises.com/free-guided-meditations-mindfulness-talks/

Mindfulness Worksheets [377]

These worksheets are free, but you can also purchase all 320 Mindfulness worksheets. [378]

Stress Eating: A Mindfulness Worksheet [379]

The Science of Mindful Eating [380]

MY FAVORITE DailyOM COURSES

28 Days to a Life of Gratitude [381]

30 Days to a Positive Money Mindset [382]

60 Meditations For Greater Happiness [383]

365 Days of Inspired Living (Brian Piergrossi) [384]

---

[377] https://mindfulnessexercises.com/free-mindfulness-worksheets/
[378] https://mindful.samcart.com/products/mindfulness-worksheets/
[379] https://mindfulnessexercises.com/stress-eating/
[380] https://mindfulnessexercises.com/the-science-of-mindful-eating/
[381] dailyom.com/cgi-bin/courses/courseoverview.cgi?cid=491
[382] dailyom.com/cgi-bin/courses/courseoverview.cgi?cid=533
[383] dailyom.com/cgi-bin/courses/courseoverview.cgi?cid=168
[384] dailyom.com/cgi-bin/courses/courseoverview.cgi?cid=151

Abundant Energy, Abundant Life [385]

Alchemical Marriage [386]

A Year of Divine Wisdom (Rasha, author of <u>Oneness</u>) [387]

A Year of Guided Meditations (Dudley and Dean Evenson) [388]

A Year of Rumi (Andrew Harvey) [389]

Becoming Happier Than God (Neale Donald Walsch) [390]

Be Your Own Guru [391]

Chakras Made Easy (Sonia Choquette) [392]

Change Your Beliefs, Change Your Life [393]

---

[385] dailyom.com/cgi-bin/courses/courseoverview.cgi?cid=729
[386] dailyom.com/cgi-bin/courses/courseoverview.cgi?cid=728
[387] dailyom.com/cgi-bin/courses/courseoverview.cgi?cid=765
[388] dailyom.com/cgi-bin/courses/courseoverview.cgi?cid=27
[389] dailyom.com/cgi-bin/courses/courseoverview.cgi?cid=35
[390] dailyom.com/cgi-bin/courses/courseoverview.cgi?cid=18
[391] dailyom.com/cgi-bin/courses/courseoverview.cgi?cid=257
[392] dailyom.com/cgi-bin/courses/courseoverview.cgi?cid=23
[393] dailyom.com/cgi-bin/courses/courseoverview.cgi?cid=609

Find Meaning Within [394]

Finding Your Way Back To You [395]

Healing Mantras for Anxiety and Depression [396]

Himalayan Wisdom for a Life Beyond Fear [397]

How to Quiet the Mind [398]

How to Meditate Without Even Trying (Peter Russell, author of <u>From Science to God: A Physicist's Journey into the Mystery of Consciousness</u> and <u>Waking Up in Time: Finding Inner Peace in Times of Accelerating Change</u>) [399]

Learning to Live (Madisyn Taylor) [400]

Master the Dao De Jing [401]

———————————————

[394] dailyom.com/cgi-bin/courses/courseoverview.cgi?cid=434
[395] dailyom.com/cgi-bin/courses/courseoverview.cgi?cid=581
[396] dailyom.com/cgi-bin/courses/courseoverview.cgi?cid=669
[397] dailyom.com/cgi-bin/courses/courseoverview.cgi?cid=448
[398] dailyom.com/cgi-bin/courses/courseoverview.cgi?cid=144
[399] dailyom.com/cgi-bin/courses/courseoverview.cgi?cid=659
[400] dailyom.com/cgi-bin/courses/courseoverview.cgi?cid=602
[401] dailyom.com/cgi-bin/courses/courseoverview.cgi?cid=252

Master the Path of the Peaceful Warrior (Dan Millman) [402]

Mastering the Energy of Money (Derek Rydall) [403]

Meditate for a More Mindful Life (Mallika Chopra) [404]

Meditation for Beginners Seminar [405]

Meditation for Spiritual Awakening [406]

Move Beyond Positive Thinking (Isha Judd, author of <u>Why Walk When You Can Fl: Soar Beyond Your Fears and Love Yourself and Others Unconditionally</u>) [407]

Navigating the Great Soul Awakening [408]

Personal Rituals for Sacred Healing (Madisyn Taylor) [409]

---

[402] dailyom.com/cgi-bin/courses/courseoverview.cgi?cid=160
[403] dailyom.com/cgi-bin/courses/courseoverview.cgi?cid=712
[404] dailyom.com/cgi-bin/courses/courseoverview.cgi?cid=700
[405] dailyom.com/cgi-bin/courses/courseoverview.cgi?cid=211
[406] dailyom.com/cgi-bin/courses/courseoverview.cgi?cid=198
[407] dailyom.com/cgi-bin/courses/courseoverview.cgi?cid=539
[408] dailyom.com/cgi-bin/courses/courseoverview.cgi?cid=141

Reinventing Happiness (Deepak Chopra and Sonja Lyubomirsky) [410]

Reinventing the Body, Resurrecting the Soul (Deepak Chopra) [411]

Rumi and the Modern Age (Andrew Harvey) [412]

Shifting from Fear to Love (Gabrielle Bernstein) [413]

Stop Being a Victim, Become a Creator (Isha Judd, author of Why Walk When You Can Fl: Soar Beyond Your Fears and Love Yourself and Others Unconditionally) [414]

Take the Journey to Authenticity [415]

The 4 Minute Peaceful Warrior Workout (Dan Millman) [416]

---

[409] dailyom.com/cgi-bin/courses/courseoverview.cgi?cid=800
[410] dailyom.com/cgi-bin/courses/courseoverview.cgi?cid=216
[411] dailyom.com/cgi-bin/courses/courseoverview.cgi?cid=122
[412] dailyom.com/cgi-bin/courses/courseoverview.cgi?cid=121
[413] dailyom.com/cgi-bin/courses/courseoverview.cgi?cid=240
[414] dailyom.com/cgi-bin/courses/courseoverview.cgi?cid=371
[415] dailyom.com/cgi-bin/courses/courseoverview.cgi?cid=457
[416] dailyom.com/cgi-bin/courses/courseoverview.cgi?cid=315

The Power of Soul: Soul Basics [417]

The Spiritual Message of the Kogi Mamos [418]

Understand that You Are Enough [419]

Unlock the Power of Chakra Magnetizing [420]

Use the Power of Mantras to Heal [421]

Visioning with Dream Boards [422]

OSHO

It is everyone's birthright to enjoy that same oceanic experience of true individuality. For that, Osho says, *There is only one path, which goes inwards, where you will not find a single human being, where you will only find silence, peace.* [423]

---

[417] dailyom.com/cgi-bin/courses/courseoverview.cgi?cid=215
[418] dailyom.com/cgi-bin/courses/courseoverview.cgi?cid=234
[419] dailyom.com/cgi-bin/courses/courseoverview.cgi?cid=519
[420] dailyom.com/cgi-bin/courses/courseoverview.cgi?cid=129
[421] dailyom.com/cgi-bin/courses/courseoverview.cgi?cid=614
[422] dailyom.com/cgi-bin/courses/co
[423] https://www.osho.com/highlights-of-oshos-world/who-is-osho

Freedom: The Courage To Be Yourself [424]

OSHO Online Library [425]

Three Types of Freedom [426]

Osho states that freedom *from* is not true freedom. To want freedom *for* (which is better than the first because you want to be free to do something), they are still aspects of the same thing.

Freedom *for* (with its more positive undertones) always has something to do with freedom *from* (which implies the negative).

The real freedom is transcendental freedom (also called *moksha*) wherein there is no goal. One simply enjoys being oneself; hence, it is an end unto itself.

---

[424] https://shop.osho.com/en/books/osho-talks/freedom
[425] https://www.osho.com/iosho/library/the-books
[426] https://s3-eu-west-1.amazonaws.com/oshonewsletter/oshonewsletter/globalenglish/jun17/what-exactly-is-freedom.html

Freedom *from* creates the politician, the reformer, the social servant, the communist, the socialist, the fascist.

Freedom *for* creates the artist, the painter, the poet, the dancer, the musician.

Transcendental freedom, for its own sake, creates the sannyasin, the mystic, the spiritual person.

Freedom *from* is very egoistic because it has to fight against something. It can be violent, in that tt has to disobey, it has to destroy, it has to conspire against the status quo.

Freedom *for* also has ego, but it is more delicate, more subtle, more profound.

In transcendental freedom, which is neither against nor for, there no ego, there no selfishness; the ego has disappeared. One has to understand the ego in order to attain this, the third freedom.

It is here that there is no need to fight for, no need to fight against; there is only just one need: to watch and be aware of how the ego functions, until the day the ego is found no more.

The ego can only exist in unawareness; when awareness comes, much like a beacon of light, the ego disappears. This is when you are able to experience transcendental freedom; the freedom without ego.

This freedom is love.

This freedom is God.

This freedom is nirvana.

This freedom is truth.

In this freedom, you exist in God and God exists in you.

This freedom is virtue wherein the very act of breathing is its own meditation.

PELMANISM

Pelmanism is a system of memory training originally devised by the Pelman Institute for the Scientific

Development of Mind, Memory, and Personality in London in the 1920s.

Pelmanism Powers [427]

The Pelman Schools [428]

THE QUANTUM WORLD

Are Subatomic Particles Vehicles of Kamma? [429]

Bohm's Gnosis: The Implicate Order [430]

Quantum Entanglement [431]

Quantum Entanglement Verified: Why Space Is Just The Construct That Gives The Illusion Of Separate Objects [432]

---

[427] http://pelmanismpowers.com

[428] www.ennever.com/histories/history386p.php

[429] https://bswa.org/forum/blogs/ed-rock/23140-are-subatomic-particles-vehicles-of-kamma

[430] www.bizint.com/stoa_del_sol/plenum/plenum_3.html

[431] https://www.sciencedaily.com/terms/quantum_entanglement.htm

[432] https://www.collective-evolution.com/2015/05/03/quantum-entanglement-verified-why-space-is-just-the-construct-that-gives-the-illusion-of-separate-objects/

Quantum Mechanics and Reality [433]

Quantum Physics [434]

Quantum Physics and Consciousness [435]

Quantum Physics and Evolving Consciousness [436]

Quantum Physics and the Afterlife [437]

Quantum Physics: An Introduction [438]

Quantum Physics, Spirituality and Your Life Experience [439]

Physics and Consciousness: Quantum Interconnectedness [440]

---

[433] www.integralscience.org/sacredscience/SS_quantum.html
[434] https://www.spaceandmotion.com/Physics-Quantum-Theory-Mechanics.htm
[435] www.markbancroft.com/info/quantum-physics-consciousness
[436] lightomega.org/Quantum-Physics-and-Evolving-Consciousness.html
[437] www.victorzammit.com/evidence/quantumphysicsdiscoveries.htm
[438] https://witnessthis.wordpress.com/2011/05/09/a-dummies-guide-to-quantum-physics/
[439] www.abundance-and-happiness.com/quantum-physics.html
[440] www.starstuffs.com/physcon/science.html

There Are No Particles, There Are Only Fields [441]

The Role of Consciousness in Quantum Physics [442]

THOUGHT

Magick of Thought: A Scientist Explores Magick [443]

TRANSFORMATIONAL TOOLS

These transformational tools have been utilized by the author whilst on her spiritual journey to **FIND HER PASSION**, **LIVE HER PURPOSE** and **MAKE AN IMPACT**.

<u>Emergence: A Revolutionary Path for Radical Life Change</u> (Derek Rydall) [444] [445]

---

[441] https://arxiv.org/ftp/arxiv/papers/1204/1204.4616.pdf

[442] whatmeditationreallyis.com/index.php/lang-en/home-blog/item/240-the-role-of-consciousness-in-quantum-physics-where-einstein-was-wrong.html

[443] www.magickofthought.com

[444] https://derekrydall.com/programs/

[445] https://itunes.apple.com/ca/podcast/emergence-revolutionary-path-for-radical-life-change/id878870353?mt=2

<u>Soul Purpose Blueprint</u> (Derek Rydall) [446]

TRANSFORMATIONAL WEBSITES

Choice Point Movement (Harry Massey) [447]

Keys to the Ultimate Freedom: Thoughts and Talks on Personal Transformation (Lester Levenson) [448]

Our Ultimate Reality [449]

Ultimate Freedom Now [450]

UDEMY COURSES

Blogging to Freedom: Create Your Independence With Blogging (Udemy Course) [451]

---

[446] https://derekrydall.com/programs/
[447] www.choicepointmovement.com
[448] www.stillnessspeaks.com/sitehtml/llevenson/keystoultimate.pdf
[449] ourultimatereality.com
[450] www.ultimatefreedomnow.com
[451] https://www.udemy.com/create-my-independence-with-blogging/

About the Author

Michele Doucette is webmistress of Portals of Spirit, a spirituality website.

As a Level 2 Reiki Practitioner, she sends long distance Reiki to those who make the request, claiming only to be a facilitator of the Universal energy, meaning that it is up to the individual(s) in question to use these energies in order to heal themselves.

Having also acquired a Crystal Healing Practitioner diploma (Stonebridge College in the UK), she is guardian to many from the mineral kingdom.

She is the author of many spiritual/metaphysical works; namely, [1] The Ultimate Enlightenment For 2012: All We Need Is Ourselves, a book that was nominated for the AllBooks Review Best Inspirational Book of 2011, [2] Turn Off The TV: Turn On Your Mind, [3] Veracity At Its Best, [4] The Collective: Essays on Reality (a composition of essays in relation to the Matrix), [5] Sleepers Awaken: The

Time Is Now To Consciously Create Your Own Reality, [6] Healing the Planet and Ourselves: How To Raise Your Vibration, [7] You Are Everything: Everything Is You, [8] The Awakening of Humanity: A Foremost Necessity, [9] The Cosmos of The Soul: A Spiritual Biography, [10] Getting Out Of Our Own Way: Love Is The Only Answer, [11] Living The Jedi Way, [12] Vicarius Christi: The Vicar of Christ, [13] A Metaphysics Primer: Changing From The Inside Out, [14] The Cosmos of The Soul II: Messages, [15] Living The ED Principles, [16] Mary Magdalene: A Personal Connection, [17] Muggle Born: Becoming The Master Magician of Your Life: Book One and [18] Muggle Born: Becoming The Master Magician of Your Life: Book Two, all of which have been published through St. Clair Publications.

In addition, she has written another volume that deals solely with crystals, aptly entitled The Wisdom of Crystals.

She is also the author of A Travel in Time to Grand Pré, a visionary metaphysical novel that historically ties the descendants of Yeshua (Jesus) to modern day Nova Scotia.

As shared by a reviewer, <u>Veracity At Its Best</u> "constructs the context for the spiritual message" imparted in <u>A Travel in Time to Grand Pré</u>.

Against the backdrop of 1754 Acadie, this novel, an alchemical tale of time travel, romance and intrigue, from Henry Sinclair to the Merovingians, from the Cathari treasure at Montségur to the Knights Templar, also blends French Acadian history with current DNA testing.

Together with the words of Yeshua as spoken at the height of his ministry, <u>A Travel in Time to Grand Pré</u> has the potential to inspire others; for it is herein that we learn how individuals can find their way, their truth(s), so as to live their lives to the fullest.

Several years in the making, she was also driven to write <u>Back Home With Evangeline</u>, the sequel to <u>A Travel in Time to Grand Pré</u>. It is here that Madeleine and Michel find themselves back in the twentieth century with a message that must be shared with the world. So, too, and even more importantly, must the message be lived, and experienced, by one and all.

So, too, is she the author of <u>Time Will Tell</u>, a uniquely moving tale that begins in the present day before weaving its way backward through time to connect a glowing thread of historic discoveries. Courtesy of past-life regression, Michaela (Dr. Mike) Callaghan, a brilliant metaphysical scientist, in the twenty-first century, discovers that she lived as a young, noble, Cathari herbalist healer, in the Languedoc area of France, during a time when political change was in the air.

The author of <u>Ad Infinitum: Unchanging and Forevermore</u>, a love story involving Ysabeau and Ghislain, twin souls who are successful in finding each other in the physical arena of the 21st century, this is a tome that delves into both incarnation (the process whereby the non-physical essence of Source is invested with physical form; a union of the physical plane of existence with the non-physical) as well as reincarnation (the re-cycling of this non-physical essence into different physical forms, different time periods and different roles, in order to experience all forms of materiality, to understand each thoroughly, and to learn how to manipulate, and maintain, these forms in balance and harmony); each is the sum total of past experiences, from various perspectives, over eons of existence.

Having retired after 31 years as a Special Education teacher, she continues to read, research and write, exploring her personal genealogies, all of which constitute her passion and contentment.

In the words of the Dalai Lama … *In order to be happy, one must first possess inner contentment; and inner contentment cannot come from having all we want; rather it comes from having and appreciating all we have.*